Fundamism

Connecting to Life Through $F.U.N.$

By

Paul J. Long

GRAB YOUR FREE GIFT!

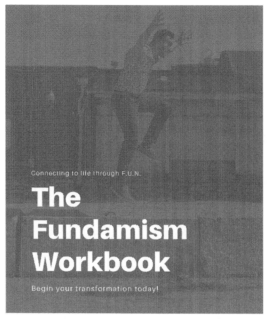

As a huge thank you for reading the book, I'd love to give you access to the downloadable, fillable PDF workbook for free.

This will help you achieve *fundamism* in your life faster and allow you space to work through the exercises at your own pace.

You can download it here:
http://pauljlong.com/freepdf

Message to the Reader

I admire you. You may be one of the countless friends, family, clients, or supporters that picked up this book to help me in my quest to guide others in finding their fundamism. Of course, you may be an individual looking to improve your own life or to find something that helps you get through a challenging moment, or maybe you just desire more fun in all you do. Either way, I admire you, and thank you for going on this journey with me.

Your decision to purchase this book is driving change for children all across the globe. A portion of all proceeds from *Fundamism: Connecting to Life Through F.U.N.* will be donated to Noah's Bandage Project to support funding for pediatric cancer research. The story of Noah Wilson, his courage and unbelievable determination to help others is featured in the book itself. However, if you want to learn more, feel free to visit www.noahsbandageproject.com.

From the bottom of my heart, I thank you and hope that fundamism guides you in finding the FUN you deserve in life.

Dedication

This book is dedicated to my amazing wife, Melissa—in the most challenging moment in my life, one where I struggled to find my own personal fun, you encouraged me to chase my dreams. As I cried on your shoulder, you advised that no amount of money is worth sacrificing my happiness. The world needs more fundamism—and you, Melissa, are the catalyst to making it happen. I love you, Bee!

I'd also like to dedicate this book to Adalyn Grace and Brennan Royal. You are two of the most fun, kind-hearted, spirited, and respectful kids any parent can ask for. I hope this book can serve as a guide and inspiration for you to help yourself and others find FUN in life. Never underestimate the difference you can make in this world. I love you, monkeys.

"**Fun** is one of the **most important**—and underrated—ingredients in any **successful venture**. If you're not having fun, then it's probably time to call it quits and **try something else**."

—*Richard Branson*

Table of Contents

Foreword
Lacing Up Your Gators

"It's not about **how to achieve your dreams**, it's about **how to lead your life...** If you lead your life **the right way**, the karma will take care of itself, the **dreams** will **come** to you."

—*Randy Pausch, professor of computer science at Carnegie Mellon University and author of **The Last Lecture***

Ever since I was a kid, I told my mom I was going to play professional sports. Growing up, I was fortunate enough to be a naturally gifted athlete.

My freshman year of college I measured 6 foot 5 inches, could run like a deer, and had great instincts on all athletic fields. Because of that, I didn't always have to work as hard as everyone else. At times, I even took things for granted.

My skillset allowed me the opportunity to play football on scholarship for the University of Cincinnati. My brother, Jason, also played football, but he didn't have the luxury of getting a free education like I did. He remains, to this day, one of the hardest workers I've ever known. I'll explain why this is relevant shortly.

I was redshirted as a freshman. That meant I got to practice with the team, but I couldn't play in games, at least not until my sophomore season, which seemed like an eternity! Not getting to play in games made me lose focus. I became a party animal. It happens to a lot of kids in their first year of college. It's your first year away from home, and you feel free. As a result, you enjoy the life you feel you were born to live.

My lack of focus jaded my perspective. I didn't use my time early on in my college career to lay the foundation of being a professional athlete. I was out enjoying life, going out throughout the week, partying hard and getting hammered. I'd go to practice hung over.

Well, life finally caught up to me...

That's one of the most important things I've learned—if you're doing the wrong things, that crap will catch up to you.

What did crap catching up to me look like?

It meant I got kicked off the team and couldn't play college sports for *365 days.*

I missed an entire year of building a resume, working on my craft, and getting better as an athlete. I had it all taken away from me due to my own negligence.

The one thing that ate me up the most was the disappointment that my parents expressed as a result of my mistakes. It killed me.

I had to make a change.

The thing is, I think everyone goes through a struggle at some point in their lives. And when it's happening, it feels like that troubled world is the only thing that exists, like you're in a rut that is impossible to get out of.

But—it always passes.

To get through it, you must understand that it's short-lived. Whatever your struggle, you've got to own it. Also, you have to realize you have the power to change it, to change your world and your worldview.

As I see it, even if something isn't under your control, the only power you have in this world is making a decision. That is it.

There's always going to be someone that's smarter, faster, stronger, more athletic, or whatever. However, no one has more power than you when you decide to make a decision. It's the only thing in your control—your decisions.

You control your decisions.

The people around me weren't getting me into trouble. It was all me. It was my decision-making. So I decided to make a new and different decision.

To get out of my negative headspace and the rut I was in I made the decision to establish a new routine. I starting waking up early and doing something productive every morning. It gave me confidence.

When I wake up early, knock out a workout, read, watch film, or listen to something motivational, it triggers my mind to attack the day and have a positive outlook on everything that comes my way. From there, I can always roll with the punches.

Around the time I began implementing my new routine was when I was first exposed to Randy Pausch's *The Last Lecture*: "If you lead your life the right way, the karma will take care of itself, the dreams will come to you." Yes, suddenly I got it. These words rang true for me.

I realized that was what my brother had been doing all along—working hard, doing the right thing, and opening lots of doors for himself, as a result. Jason's tenacity and tireless effort in achieving his goals played a critical role most recently in allowing him the opportunity to win a Super Bowl while playing center for the Philadelphia Eagles.

In order to fulfill my childhood dream of becoming a professional athlete, I decided to start leading life the right way. I began working on me, gravitating towards the things that I love and starting the search to find my authentic self.

The second decision I made to get through the most challenging time in my life was to find something else, besides football that I loved and found incredibly fun.

I started playing summer baseball.

Finding that something you love to do, that's super fun, allows you to focus on your present and future rather than on your past mistakes or disappointments. Find something that you enjoy and do it often. I didn't know it at the time, but this concept is the basis for the book you're reading now. It's Paul Long's philosophy of *fundamism*: don't wallow in the bad stuff from the past because it keeps you stuck; instead, regularly do what you truly enjoy, so you keep positive, content, and moving forward.

Just because I found what Paul Long calls *fundamism* doesn't mean that I don't fall victim to regression from time to time. Challenges still come, and it takes practice and diligence to make it through them. Despite the fact that I made a decision to live genuinely and "lead my life the right way," I distinctly remember moments where I found myself losing sight of what the "right way" actually was.

My first couple of years in the league, there were times where I was trying to portray an image that wasn't me. On the field, I'm always a competitor, in the zone. But off the field, I was trying to be someone that everyone liked. By doing that, I started to fall away from my authentic self.

Pleasing everyone is not possible.

That time in my career pushed me away from many of the individuals that I hold near and dear to me, folks that always supported me. Why? Because I was trying to be something I wasn't. Getting back to my genuine self has allowed me to find my strength again, and I'm comfortable knowing whoever accepts me, accepts the real me.

Today, I'm in a much better place than I was when I was younger. I wake up, and I appreciate everything that comes my way. That's the fun of it. That's life at its best.

Even if you plan something fun to do, you never know how it's going to end up. But if you appreciate everything that comes your way and you roll with the curves that life presents you, fun will begin finding you, rather than you having to seek it out.

Rick Flair once said, "I'm having a hard time holding these alligators down." He was referencing his shoes, but I believe there's a metaphor in there for how to live life. Rick Flair's confidence, hard work, and ownership mentality created a wealth of opportunity for him. By limiting excuses in life and having the confidence that you can achieve anything, you too will have a hard time holding those alligators down. Once you lace those gators up, they'll want to run wild. Once you find your true authentic self, anything is possible, and personal freedom is within your reach. How wild is that?

In addition to appreciating everything that comes my way, I also believe in consistent self-development. Growing as an individual can help drive improvements in how you handle future adversity in life.

I'm always working to be the best football player I can be, but that's not enough. I want to be a better person, as well. The one thing I'd like to continue to work on is my intellect. I didn't always take school as seriously as I should have.

My father can watch *Jeopardy* and ramble off answers to all the questions. Oftentimes, I find myself wondering, "I have that in my genes?! What am I friggin' doing here? I'm sitting here clueless about everything Alex Trebek is asking!"

Consistent self-development is important in improving your quality of life. I'm working to better my knowledge of the world, the surroundings around me, and to expose myself to things that will support mental growth.

What's the one thing you'd like to improve in your life?

As you progress through *Fundamism: Connecting to Life Through F.U.N.*, you're going to have many opportunities to self-reflect and self-develop. In talking to Paul, I know I did.

As you reflect, find comfort in revisiting the past. Yes, you'll feel some pain but reliving how you felt through your worst moments can help keep you on track. It keeps your mind in a place where you're motivated to make sure you never get back to that point again.

The key to growth is pushing through the heartache without wallowing in it and developing a plan to move yourself forward. Find your fun, what Paul calls your "FUNdamentals."

My FUNdamentals are rooted in routine, self-improvement, authenticity, and enjoyment—leading my life the right way and letting the karma take care of itself.

What will yours look like?

Everyone is going through something. As the dark is revealed, the sun will come out again. Every day is a new day, and you can attack it as such. As challenging as it may seem to make it through, you will. You have before, and you'll do it again.

The one thing you can control is your decisions. You can decide to put *fundamism* into practice, to find your FUNdammentals, and invest in the journey of this book. I've already made those decisions, and what I've found as a result—life sure has been a whole lot more FUN!

—*Travis Kelce, All-Pro Tight End for the Kansas City Chiefs*

Introduction
Get Your F.U.N. On!

"We **don't stop playing** because we grow old; we grow old because we stop playing."

—George Bernard Shaw

Identify someone in your life that consistently appears upbeat, optimistic, and troubled by nothing. On the surface, they seem to truly enjoy life and have FUN in all they do. Take a moment and recall that person . . .

Have you ever wished you could be a little more like them? Wished that you could let things roll off you like the water off a duck's back? Jump for no reason? Sing out loud without worrying what others think? Create games out of mundane tasks? Incorporate a little more FUN in your life?

Great news—you can! By reading this book you're one step closer to connecting to life through F.U.N.!

Vulnerability and acceptance are paramount in achieving growth. In order for joy and fulfillment to become the defining elements of your life, you have to accept and move forward from any past experiences that may be holding you back. Are you truly committed to creating change in how you experience life? Are you willing to do what's necessary to have more FUN in life? Before we discuss how to get there, let's explore some of the experiences that could be keeping you from the contentment you deserve.

What do you recall being the most challenging time in your life? Close your eyes and picture the heartache or anxiety you felt. Maybe you lost a job, went through a terrible breakup, didn't know how you were going to pay the bills, were diagnosed with a life-altering ailment, or experienced the passing of a loved one? Whatever the challenge, recollect how it felt like there was no way you could get through that difficult time.

We all desire happiness, and minimal stress. However, life doesn't care what we want. And, life doesn't always work out as we plan. To truly maximize life experience, all we can do is live with purpose and learn from our experiences—which is not the same as dwelling on them. The shorter the memory we have when it comes to those challenges we've faced, coupled with a strong ability to quickly move through painful situations, will help determine how joy-filled our experience in life will be.

Now let's revisit that particularly challenging moment in your life. At the time, you thought life was running circles around you and you couldn't see the end of the super tough situation. You probably wanted to give up, were overwhelmed with emotions, and were stressed all the time. You thought there was no possible way you could make it through the pain and trouble. But—you did.

Here you are—today, right now—taking the first step in bringing more fun, fulfillment, and joy to your life. The thing you thought couldn't be done, you did. Challenges will continue to come. However, in reading *Fundamism: Connecting to Life Through F.U.N.* you are preparing yourself with the practices, habits, tools, and techniques necessary to combat the negative headspace such challenges create. You are moving yourself forward in finding your FUN!

Just That Simple

Back in 1991, a boxer by the name of Vinny Pazienza was riding the ultimate high. He was working on reinventing himself as more of a strategic boxer rather than the brawler he once was. Vinny saw a championship fight just within reach. But, life didn't work out as he had planned. What happened? A horrific car accident brought Vinny's dream to a screeching halt.

Vinny awoke with doctors and family by his side. He was advised that he'd broken his neck in the accident and was given two options in recovery. The first option was spinal fusion surgery. The second was a metal halo screwed into his skull and other areas of the body to immobilize his neck. Vinny went the route of the halo as he felt it provided him a higher probability of success in living the life he'd once lived.

"When can I fight again?" Vinny asked the doctor.

"I'm not sure you're understanding the severity of the situation, Vinny," the doctor answered. "We're not certain you'll ever walk again, so fighting is almost an uncertainty."

Vinny's response: he was certain at that moment that he'd fight again. And fight he did. Vinny worked tirelessly for a return to the ring, even working out while wearing the halo.

Fourteen months following the car crash, Vinny was back in the ring boxing again. He ultimately beat the best pound-for-pound boxer in the world, Roberto Duran, and held a championship belt again.

In the movie *Bleed for This* there's an interview with Vinny Pazienza that happened several weeks after his fight with Duran. A reporter asked Vinny what he learned through his experience.

Vinny answered, "I learned that people will tell you all sorts of lies to get ahead in the world."

"What's the biggest lie you've ever been told?" the reporter asked.

"It's not that simple," Vinny said.

"What do you mean, 'It's not that simple'?" responded the reporter.

"No, that's the biggest lie I've ever been told—*it's not that simple*," Vinny explained.

We've all heard that statement: "It's not that simple." I'm certain we've all said it a few times in our own lives:

- I want a better job, but . . . *it's not that simple.*

- I want more money, but . . . *it's not that simple.*

- I want to deal with this crippling anxiety, but . . . *it's not that simple.*

- I want to experience more fun in life, but . . . *it's not that simple.*

"It *is* that simple," Vinny went on to say. "Do the thing they say can't be done, then it's done. Then you realize—it *is* that simple and it always was."

The purpose of this book is to mitigate the sting of challenging times, identify the things that give you strength in life, and provide direction on how to gravitate towards them. If you want to live a life filled with more joy, fun, and fulfillment, it is that simple. Stop focusing on what's not working and create more of what does work. Whether you're an individual wanting to experience life in a different light or an organization with the goal of creating a fun, employee-focused culture, you've taken the first step in accomplishing your goal. Welcome to *Fundamism: Connecting to Life Through F.U.N.*

As I see it, fun is an experience that is underappreciated and easily created. It's underappreciated because so many of us forget the monumental role having fun can play in shifting our mindset from one of heartache or dismay to one of joy and satisfaction. Fun is easily created because everyone on this planet has something they do for fun, and with a little thought we can turn even the most monotonous of tasks into something enjoyable. *Fundamism: Connecting to Life Through F.U.N.* will guide you on how to establish a joy-based mindset and a fun-based life, both at work, at home, and anywhere else your experiences take you.

The F.U.N. of Fundamism

Fundamism is the philosophy of purposefully living a fun and fulfilling life. The F.U.N. of fundamism is an acronym representing the three key aspects of the philosophy. F.U.N. reminds us to focus on consistently building a personal *foundation*, striving to *understand others' perspectives*, and identifying *next steps* to ensure we're all living our best life while maximizing the experience. In the pages that follow, you'll learn about fundamism in detail so that you can set your happy-machine on full-blast. Here are some areas we'll be exploring:

F = Foundation

If you consider yourself purpose-driven, what is your purpose? How does this purpose manifest itself in all you do? If you were to describe yourself in three words, what would they be? How do those three words align with how others describe you?

Your personal foundation is everything that makes you, you. Your purpose in life, personality style, ability to communicate effectively, and the experiences that have shaped you help establish how you experience life. If you sincerely desire fun and satisfaction in life, you must take a deep look inside yourself to identify where your strengths and areas of opportunities lie. The foundation chapter of this book will guide you in clearly identifying your personal foundation, reveal areas that can be improved, and help to create alignment in your life.

U = Understanding Others' Perspectives

What drives the differences between us? Why do we connect with some individuals better than others? Do you find that you're typically "curious" or "furious" in situations where someone rubs you the wrong way? How do you create more meaningful interactions?

Understanding others' perspectives is critical in maximizing joy and contentment in life. Taking the time to walk in the shoes of others will enable you to create more positive, memorable experiences in your journey. This is what the U in F.U.N. is all about!

N = Next Steps

You've explored your foundation and feel you're on the right track in understanding the perspective of others. What's next? What are the tactical things that you can do right now to drive more fun and fulfillment in life?

Next Steps allows you to immerse yourself in activities and behaviors that will actually generate change in your life. If you want to have more fun in life, *next steps* is where the rubber truly meets the road.

Setting Yourself Free of "Woe Is Me"

We all know people that brighten up a room when they enter. In contrast, I'm sure many of you know folks that when they LEAVE the room, the room brightens up a little! The question then becomes—which are you? With whom do your surround yourself?

We've all played the victim a few times in our lives. Even the happiest of people have bad days. We talk to ourselves and say things like:

- "No one has it as bad as I do."

- "What difference can I make?"

- "My day would go better if others would pull their head out of their ass!"

- "Why does God hate me?"

- "Everything bad in life happens to me."

Do any of these excuses sound familiar?

Throughout my tenure in many positions of leadership, I've heard many excuses about why someone is grumpy or angry in life. Many have said that past experiences help develop a person's attitude. Those who lose loved ones or suffer through bad relationships struggle with getting close to others. Those who continuously get the short end of the stick expect the shaft and actually begin to anticipate its arrival.

I get all of this. To tell you the truth, I agree that sometimes life is not fair. Unfortunately for us, life does not give a damn. Life does not stop to cry about what has happened nor does life stop to admire what has been accomplished. Successes or failures are all based on the human mind and a person's own perspective. It is important to know that your path is already set in motion. The responsibility of paving it and minimizing bumps along the way lies squarely on your shoulders. But that doesn't mean you have to walk it alone.

Fundamism: Connecting to Life Through F.U.N. is here to act as your guide, your map, and your playbook so that you not only have an easier time minimizing those bumps—you'll experience fun and satisfaction along the way. This book supplies you with a ton of options, inspiring real-life stories, research-based recommendations, realistic and doable advice, and a wide range of practice activities—so that you'll have the guidance and support you need to establish a positive, joy-based mindset and a fun and fulfilling life.

There's no time like the present to get in on the fun! First stop on the journey: to help any of you still stuck in your "woe is me" excuses, I tell the unlikely story of how I landed on fundamism.

Chapter 1
Arriving at Fun's Front Door

"I will love the **light** for it **shows me the way**, yet I will endure the **darkness** for it **shows me the stars**."

—*Og Mandino*

To give you some important background on fundamism—and to establish some essential elements of the fundamism philosophy of living—let me tell you how I arrived at fun's front door. Simply put—pain. Pain, disappointment, sadness, and injustice—that's what propelled me to embrace fun and all that fun has to offer. As contrary as it may sound, it was all things negative in life that convinced me that fun is the way to go. Let me give you the stories, so you can get that much closer to embracing fundamism, no matter the hurt and disappointment you may have experienced.

Victim or Victor: The Choice

Growing up was easy for me. Despite the fact that my parents divorced shortly after I reached the age of one, I was truly blessed with friends and family that loved me, unconditionally. Both my mother and father remarried, and while my mother's second marriage was short-lived, my father's endured the test of time.

Like many, we struggled with money. I distinctly remember situations where I had to go to the grocery store and buy milk with food stamps. Or the time I was asked by my mother to take a Ziploc bag of nickles and dimes into the gas station to put five dollars of gas in our rusty Oldsmobile Delta Eighty-Eight.

Throughout the early years of my adolescence, I didn't fully understand how amazing my stepmother truly was. At times, I looked at her as the "wicked witch of the Midwest" and even convinced myself that my story paralleled that of Cinderella. Of course, I mean a more burly, boss-dude, masculine version of Cinderella, but Cinderella nevertheless. My friends would always joke around about the chores I had to do before I could hang out. "Hey, Paul, we would ask you to go to the football game, but you wouldn't have enough time to paint the house," they would joke.

Every time I asked my father if I could stay the night at my friend John's, he would respond with the same old tired line, "Yeah, you can go, just not today." This would then be followed by the most annoying laugh you ever heard.

It wasn't until after I graduated high school that I realized my stepmother was the glue that held our whole family together. Our family consisted of my father, stepmother, brother, two half-sisters, and me.

As I'm sure you can imagine, feeding a family of six wasn't always the easiest. My stepmother worked in the claims department at WalMart and my father worked (when he was able to) as a building official for the City of Louisburg, Kansas.

I love my father. He is my blood and has helped me to become everything that I am today. He did this by modeling the traits I wanted to emulate while also showing me things I never wanted to become. We all have strengths and opportunity gaps. When you closely observe all sides of a person, it is possible to learn and grow from almost all individuals in your life.

Choosing "Victim"

My father suffered from a debilitating disease that millions of people suffer from around the world. Some are able to recover. They surround themselves with positive people and a support system that aids them in overcoming the sickness. Others are not so fortunate. They allow the disease to define their existence and negatively impact those around them. This disease is spreading rampantly throughout our planet. While the sickness may not have an official medical term, it can adequately be described in three words: WOE IS ME!!!!

My father was an entrepreneur who made a living developing commercial buildings in the Kansas City area. He was on cloud nine after landing one of his largest jobs to date when he began the lengthy and expensive process of constructing a new development. However, the company that hired my father had been experiencing financial instability and ended up filing bankruptcy.

After this happened, the world that my father knew was sent into a tailspin. Everything that he owned was tied to this development, so he lost thousands and thousands of dollars. At this point he had to make a choice. He could use this experience as a growth opportunity for himself, or he could make it an excuse and highlight it as the defining moment in a life that didn't turn out as expected. Ultimately, this moment was the beginning of my father's demise—a downward spiral plagued by addiction and reoccurring back problems caused, in my opinion, by immersing himself in a lifetime of negative baggage.

My father filed bankruptcy in his thirties, and it negatively impacted his life ever since. He blamed every failure or loss on that one experience and had trouble owning outcomes based on his decisions. Shortly after my father's sixtieth birthday, he passed. The last five years of his life he spent sleeping exclusively in a recliner, in a fog created by opiates, and consuming a diet that consisted mainly of Milky Way Simply Caramel bars and Coca-Cola, while lighting each new cigarette with the previous one. He gave up on life but sought forgiveness from those around him.

Life does not always happen as we've planned for it to happen. Many of us have experienced horrible things that no one person should have to see or feel. These experiences, however, help define who we are and what we become. The strength that we possess and develop through times of sorrow becomes a part of us and allows others to see that recovery is possible.

I forgive him. My father's suffering gave me the ability to thrive. His strengths shaped me. His opportunities drove me. I am thankful for every experience that he went through because it gave me the fire to help others overcome the hardships they face.

My dad was special, as are you. Don't give up. There's still time to make the changes necessary to create more happiness in your life.

Choosing "Victor"

I now realize that my stepmother is truly a saint. She is one of two unbelievable moms in my life, and I don't consider her a stepmother at all. To me, she is just mom. Mom managed the family finances and limited the negative impact our father could play on our attitudes by showing my siblings and me that we had a choice. She could have allowed herself to fall into the "funk" that plagued my father on a regular basis. However, she remained as strong as Sylvester Stallone in his arm-wrestling classic, *Over the*

Top, and continues to be one of the most optimistic people I have ever met.

You have a choice. You can be the example of what those around you are scared to death to become, or you can be an inspiration to others. This can only be done by the way you choose to react to life experiences. Life doesn't stop to cry about what has happened, so why should we spend too much time doing so?

It is perfectly acceptable to grieve, reflect, and express sadness in times of heartache. Tears are good for the healing process, and I encourage everyone to shed a few during difficult times. However, if you are both determined and quick to look ahead and move forward, you will find it impossible to drown in the puddles those tears leave.

The examples my father and stepmother set certainly paved my way to fundamism, but what landed me on fun's doorstep is another story—the story of Noah Wilson.

Noah—Courageous, Present, Impactful

Did you know that only 4% of federal cancer funding supports pediatric cancer research? I didn't either until I was introduced to one of the most caring, wise, funny, strong, driven, and inspirational people I've ever met. I'd like to call your attention to the fact that the individual exhibiting those traits—who started a charity founded on giving hope to those in need, inspired an entire community to raise awareness for pediatric cancer research, and altered the course of my life—this individual was only seven years old. His name is Noah Wilson.

What does charity, community, pediatric cancer, and little Noah Wilson have to do with fundamism? In short, the story of Noah Wilson became the inspiration I needed to finish the book you're reading now. People ask me all the time why I'm so passionate about pediatric cancer research and the events that led to me becoming president of the Noah's Bandage Project Board. In the pages that follow, you'll learn that Noah Wilson not only embodied many elements of fundamism, he is the blueprint for how fundamism can be leveraged to help change your perspective and bring more happiness to your life.

To understand the depth of this incredible boy, the courage he showed, and the impact he left on this earth, it's important to learn his story from someone with firsthand knowledge and experience. Unfortunately, Noah Wilson passed at the age of seven. He'll never fully understand the difference he made to Scott (his father), Deb (his mother), his siblings, or the countless others he inspired. However, by reading the following words of Scott Wilson, my hope is that you find strength in Noah's story and are driven to alter the narrative in your own:

Noah was always an "easy" child. From the moment he was born, he always had an incredible peace about him and a confidence that he could do anything. When he walked into a room, a peace would fill the space. He loved God and was confident in his calling. We believe this confidence is what helped him remain so courageous throughout his life.

In March of 2014, Noah began experiencing pain in his lower back and right leg. It started off as an intermittent pain throughout the day that seemed to worsen at night. He had trouble sleeping flat in his bed, so he and I would camp out on the recliner in our family room. We started the process of getting him checked out by a doctor, visiting a chiropractor, urgent care, and even the ER over the course of about a month. The pain would come and go but eventually got worse, to the point that it hurt to walk, twist, and even move.

This was the start of Noah's courage. Despite his pain, he still smiled when he could. He put up with a month-long process of trying to figure out what was going on and never lost his spirit of peace.

On April 18, 2014, at the age of six, Noah was diagnosed with cancer. It was in his back, on his T12 vertebrae, and was wrapping itself around his spine. The pressure from the tumor pressing against his spinal cord was what was causing the pain in his lower back and leg.

Over the next week, Noah was poked and prodded, and he underwent biopsies, procedures, MRIs, CT scans, bone scans, and PET scans. All of it was scary, and most required him to be sedated. He was put under almost every day for a week, sometimes multiple times in a day. He was going through terrifying events, and we were doing everything we could to stay positive and show him strength. Who knew? It was Noah, wise beyond his years, providing us strength the whole time.

With every procedure, while Noah was scared, he would do everything the doctors asked. He would walk into hospital rooms without us and later wake up in a daze not knowing where he was and press his morphine button repeatedly to try and keep the pain from being unbearable. Despite this, we would see his smile every night as we prayed and asked God to heal him.

Noah was officially diagnosed with Ewing's sarcoma, a bone cancer that represents about 6% of all pediatric cancer cases. There are roughly 200 children per year in the United States diagnosed with this form of cancer, so it is considered to be extremely rare. He stared chemotherapy on April 25, 2014.

Early on into his chemo treatments, Noah would get shots in his legs every night. The shots provided him a steroid that would help counteract the impacts of the chemo drugs. Chemotherapy is very hard on the body, especially that of children. One night following his shots, Noah asked his nurse if they had any superhero bandages, rather than the traditional, boring brown bandages they had been giving him. You could see the disappointment in his eyes when the nurse told him that that was all they had. The disappointment quickly morphed into inspiration, and we could tell Noah had an idea.

Noah knew what these bandages meant to kids. They were more than just a means to cover their wounds. Rather, they were a badge of courage. A badge to show others that you overcame the anxiety and pain of something incredibly scary.

A bandage could help kids identify one another too by displaying a child's individual interests, likes, and hobbies. Noah observed that kids on his floor all wore the same hospital gowns and many were bald, so everyone looked the same. They needed something different, a differentiator, and that's what bandages offered.

We'll never forget the determined look Noah expressed when he entered our room one afternoon with a sign he'd made entirely on his own. It read, "If you have any Band-Aids, put them in this basket for Children's Mercy." He told us that he wanted to start collecting bandages so that all kids at the hospital could have cool, fun "badges" to help them get better. This was the beginning of Noah's Bandage Project.

With the help of our friends and local news outlets, word spread quickly of Noah's quest to find fun bandages. His project took off and people from all over the world wanted to help. We received boxes from California, New York, Ohio, and even England. Noah's work didn't stop with bandages though. With only 4% of federal funding going to pediatric cancer research, Noah wanted to help advance treatments and provide additional hope to the young warriors battling this terrible disease. In just over two years, Noah's Bandage Project collected over 67 thousand boxes of fun bandages and generated in excess of $350,000 for pediatric cancer research!

Noah consistently showed a genuine interest in others—not just through the work of his project, but in his daily interactions as well. One day at the hospital, Noah met a teenage girl by the name of Brittany. Brittany, a fellow cancer warrior, had to get a feeding tube placed in her nose similar to Noah's. Cancer treatments impact the whole body. The chemotherapy drugs not only attack the cancer but attack the healthy parts of the body causing most patients to lose a lot of weight. Some, like Noah and Brittany, lose their appetites altogether.

Brittany didn't come out of her room much due to the embarrassment she felt after receiving her newly placed feeding tube. The tube was visible to others and, in her opinion, did not look "normal." On this particular day, Noah was playing in the playroom when Brittany decided to come get a movie to take back to her room. She saw Noah with his feeding tube doing some crafts. Noah immediately struck up a conversation with her.

The conversation quickly led to their feeding tubes with Brittany asking questions about how he liked it and what others thought. Noah glowed when communicating how the tube allowed him to take meds without the horrible taste and how he could eat his food without doing any work. In this way, this six-year-old boy was encouraging a teenage girl not to be afraid and was helping her identify the good that comes with a feeding tube.

This was Noah. He carried with him a spirit created to help. Being appreciative of what has been given, showing a genuine interest in others, providing hope to those in need, and smiling through it all defined our little boy. He was taken from this earth on June 30, 2015, after developing a secondary form of cancer known as leukemia.

Noah never let his cancer diagnosis stop him from fulfilling the plan we feel God had for him. He looked cancer in the face and said, "I will not be afraid of you. You will not stop me from helping others." This is the mindset that we carry in our continued work with Noah's Bandage Project, and it is our hope that his story inspires you to do the same in your life.

I had the pleasure of meeting Noah Wilson in April of 2015. He was a huge Kansas City Royals fan, and apparently, he appreciated the silliness of the catsuits my friend John Stoner (yes, Stoner) and I were wearing (more to follow).

I'll never forget the day Noah and I connected. Noah's father, Scott, invited John and me to the hospital for a brief visit as Noah was undergoing treatment. This was my first trip to the pediatric wing of any hospital, and I was overcome with emotion.

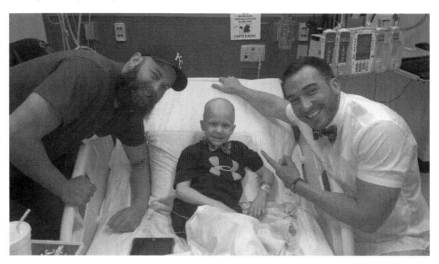

When we entered Noah's room, Scott greeted us. He mentioned that Noah was pretty worn out but excited to meet us. As I glanced over at Noah, I felt a reluctance from him about our visit. My heart was heavy, and I worried that Noah didn't want us there. Really though, this was my mind deciding to take on a negative perspective (you know—choosing "victim" over "victor").

So often I find that our preconceived notions of how an experience will play out get in the way of our experiencing things as they truly are playing out. Often we limit opportunities in life based on how we FEEL things are going to go. We get an idea about a situation and let it determine how we experience it (no matter how far from reality our idea is). However, the truth is, we have no idea how things are going to go, so the best way to handle it is to be present and choose to stay positive! As you'll soon learn, this is a foundational component of fundamism.

The feeling that Noah didn't want us there was something I'd concocted in my head. Because I was uncomfortable and scared of seeing my own children go through what Noah was experiencing, I put that energy on him and the situation—and determined that he was unhappy with the visit.

My feelings of discomfort quickly subsided when Noah and I began chatting. The moment I got out of my head, became present in the experience, and was able to feel Noah's calm and positive energy, was the moment our connection sparked.

Noah and I immediately began talking about the Kansas City Royals, a team that would later make its first MLB postseason appearance in 29 years. Noah's face lit up. He began asking questions about our catsuits and our favorite Royals players, while showing a genuine interest in us both.

As I stood there chatting with this amazing boy, I couldn't help but appreciate the moment. Here was Noah decked out in a black Under Armour shirt, beautiful bald head, and a smile that could light up any metropolitan area. This kid was battling cancer, undergoing chemotherapy, and appeared absolutely exhausted lying in his hospital bed. Despite all of this, I never heard one negative word out of his mouth, and he seemed completely present in the moment. I could learn from him.

As John and I prepared to leave, we gave Noah an awesome custom bowtie featuring the Hulk to symbolize our appreciation of his strength and courage. Several hours after our departure, we received a group text from Scott Wilson. The message remains one of the most memorable gifts anyone has ever given me: a video of Noah Wilson. Noah stood in the hospital hallway, connected to an IV. With a smile on his face, waving a blue Royals towel over his head, and sporting his newly acquired bowtie, he cheerfully exclaimed, "Gooooooo Royals! Thanks cat guys for coming. See you soon!" Tears streamed down my face as I watched the video multiple times.

Noah Wilson will always have a special place in my heart. Over the next few months I was inspired by his silly YouTube videos, the desire he expressed daily to help others, and his love of baseball. I even got to attend his first little league baseball game in over a year as he underwent his final stages of chemotherapy. This was a game where he went 2 for 3 from the dish and had a putout at first. The delight he carried with him from playing this game was tremendous and something none of us will ever understand. Seeing him struggle running around the bases, clearly in pain and exhaustion due to his treatment, will forever be etched in my mind. Despite my perspective of how terrible he must have felt, Noah exuded happiness, excitement, and gratitude during this experience. He was completely in the moment. Talk about a joy-filled perspective!

Noah changed my life. He provided me the perspective and direction that I'd been lacking for years. I was with him the day he passed and am eternally grateful that his family invited me to the hospital to say goodbye. This day marked the end of his pain and the beginning of his amazing legacy.

To understand the concept of fundamism and the power perspective can hold on our mindset, I found it essential to share Noah's story. While his story is unbelievably sad, Noah found peace and strength in his purpose. A purpose he knew was defined by bringing happiness and hope to others. His purpose helped frame the pain he felt, encouraged him to fight, and gave his parents the strength they needed to carry forward. The mentality he carried—focusing on what gave him strength as opposed to what tore him down—defines fundamism.

As you progress through the remainder of this book and begin implementing fundamism in your life, remember that perspective is everything. No matter your circumstance, there will always be someone that has it worse than you. Quite honestly, they might even be handling it better and finding deep purpose in their pain like little Noah Wilson.

Find inspiration in Noah's life story, alter your perspective, gravitate towards the things that give you strength, and appreciate the amazing things you have in life. In doing so, I promise your mindset will transform and additional opportunity—plus greater delight and fulfillment—will reveal itself.

FUN Chapter Takeaways

- You have a choice: victim or victor.

- Perspective is everything. Your perspective on a situation and on your life as a whole doesn't just happen. It's something you choose.

- Draw inspiration from the joy-filled, purpose-driven perspective Noah chose to embrace.

Next Up

I know what you're thinking, "Wait, is this dude just going to glance over the fact that two guys were prancing around in catsuits? What exactly is a 'catsuit'?" In the next chapter you'll learn the full story of how John Stoner and I became the Kansas City Royals' Fans of the Year once we got out of our heads, stopped worrying about what people thought of us, and had a ton of fun. This "catsuit craze" will serve as part of our larger discussion of daily purposeful engagement in fun, aka FUNdamentals.

Chapter 2
The FUNdamentals of Fundamism

"You probably **wouldn't worry** about what people think of you if you could know how seldom they do."

—*Olin Miller*

Having a victim's mentality never got my father anywhere. In fact, it drove a wedge between him and others to such a point that he couldn't connect with many people and cultivate the personal relationships he desired. Knowing that everyone goes through challenges in life, what can we do differently to ease the pain these challenges create? What can we do to make the most out of every minute?

People who exude happiness and positivity typically have many commonalities. One commonality is their ability to incorporate certain FUNdamentals on a daily basis. These FUNdamentals allow them to focus on the future and forget about the drama that tends to keep us from realizing true happiness. This is a concept known as "forward-thinking." Forward-thinking is based on the notion that we cannot change the past, we can only influence or impact the future. By finding things that help us to focus on the good in life, we can more readily move on from difficult or trying times.

Someone that I look up to very much in life once told me that if I wanted to be successful, I should mirror what other successful people do. That same principle can be applied to changing our perspective on life. If we want to be more positive and live fulfilling lives, let's do what other positive individuals do! That's where the FUNdamentals of fundamism come in.

Fundamism can be defined as the FUNdamentals of a FUN and optimistic lifestyle. These FUNdamentals are anything that you gravitate towards that provide you with strength, happiness, or mental release. When you're having a bad day and it seems nothing is going right, what do you do to overcome that negative headspace? Oftentimes when I ask this question to groups, common responses are hanging with the family, playing with kids, or going out to eat with a loved one. While these are all FUNdamentals and can be fantastic experiences, relying on the presence of others to provide strength can create significant problems down the road. Let me explain.

Have you ever wondered what makes breakups so challenging? If you've experienced a terrible breakup in the past, I'm sure you can relate to the roller coaster of emotions that soon followed. Why? Is it because we feel a sense of failure, rejection, or sadness that comes along when a large chapter of our life comes to an end? Those are all good answers. However, I believe that the biggest struggle after a breakup is finding strength in yourself again, without the dependency of others.

Relationships come with sacrifice, which means that many of the things we did for FUN before getting together, are exchanged for more couple-friendly activities. The same phenomenon can take place once children enter the mix. This is perfectly acceptable and natural in life's cycle. Where it can become a problem is when you lose a part of your identity and lack the ability to find things that give you strength without the help of others.

Challenge yourself to come up with five or more things you do for FUN without depending on others now and write them down below. These are your FUNdamentals! How many more can you come up with?

1. _____

2. _____

3. _____

4. _____

5. _____

Meditating, singing aloud, exercise, listening to music with purpose, enjoying a great meal, dressing up in a funny costume, going for a walk, and playing a board game can all be considered FUNdamentals. There are a million of them out there but not every FUNdamental will be FUN for you.

Throughout this book, I'll provide you many examples of FUNdamentals that have worked for others and myself in our lives. The purpose is not to have every FUNdamental appeal to you, but rather to provoke thought and drive you to incorporate more of those that give you strength into your daily life. By implementing FUNdamentals daily as other positive people do, we can realize our own potential in leading the you-filled life we all desire.

The Catsuit Craze

What's your biggest fear? Snakes? Public speaking? Perhaps you're like Dwayne "the Rock" Johnson's character in the movie *Central Intelligence* and you are petrified of people seeing you naked? Think about your fear for a second … Got it?

Now think about experiencing that fear and having your reaction exposed on a stage with millions of people watching. This was the situation I found myself in when my best friend convinced me to do something bold.

The date was June 8 in the year of my Kansas City Royals' resurrection, 2014. Derek Jeter and his New York Yankees traveled to Kauffman Stadium, home of the Kansas City Royals. Kauffman was also my best buddy, John Stoner's and my favorite weekend getaway. Jeter announced his intention to retire at season's end and was in the middle of his farewell tour. Fans in every Major League city were coming out to celebrate Derek Jeter's storied career, coming up with creative ways to say goodbye while thanking him for being an ambassador to America's favorite pastime. John and I would not be outdone.

Weeks prior while surfing the interwebs, John found some ridiculously outlandish wrestling singlets featuring a large profile pic of a cat on the front and back. He called me immediately.

John: You'll never guess what I found.

Me: You're right.

John: Did you know they made cat wrestling singlets with cat profile pics on them?

Me: How would I possibly know that?

John: Great point . . . I bought two.

Me: What could we possibly use those for?

John: I don't know, but it's going to be AWESOME!

One day while watching ESPN, we found our answer. Fans in every Major League city were showing out in celebration of Derek Jeter's storied career.

"Eureka!" John exclaimed.

What environment wouldn't be infinitely improved with the addition of two dudes in cat wrestling singlets, or "catsuits" as they would later be identified? For those of you who aren't familiar with a wrestling singlet—think lycra bodysuit with the leg section extending just above the knee and the upper body section sleeveless, like a tank top. And, yes, our singlets featured huge cat profile pictures on the front and back...hence, "catsuit."

We bought our tickets to the June 8 Royals vs. Yankees game, and suited up in our ridiculous outfits.

Full disclosure—I'm not deathly afraid of making a fool of myself. John and I had made the world our stage for years and were no strangers to folks laughing at our shenanigans.

However, if you're not a man, you may not understand the complex that young boys create for one another in the locker rooms of elementary school.

Regardless of whether one is "gifted" or not, many boys often wonder how they stack up against others and are afraid to learn the answer. While I wasn't afraid of making a fool of myself, the thought of my kibbles and bits being exposed to the masses via the oh-so-snug-fitting lycra created a little anxiety.

Away we went. Sporting our silly catsuits, John and I made signs "littered" with cat puns, such as, "Derek Jeter, One Classy Cat," and "Strike 'Em Out Right Meow." With signs in hand and bodies exposed, we headed to Kaufmann Stadium.

As we walked into the venue, we were greeted immediately with laughter. However, a funny thing happened. The laughter was soon accompanied by high-fives, smiles, and awesome comments. Don't get me wrong, there were some rude people who didn't have very nice things to say. Matter of fact, some had some downright awful things to say. These people were in the minority and will exist in any situation, but they were quickly drowned out by those celebrating our boldness.

Soon, folks began coming up to us requesting pictures. Oh, the pictures! We took well over a hundred pics that day and wound up being tagged in Facebook photos of people all over the Kansas City community. We made an appearance on the JumboTron, were featured on live TV multiple times while dancing in the stands, were interviewed live on a local Fox morning news program, and were written up in publications around the nation.

Can you imagine the pride my mother exuded when I told her I was featured in the Washington Post, Yahoo Sports, and even in a full-page article in the Wall Street Journal? Can you then imagine the subsequent disappointment she had when I explained why we were in said publications?

Several people commented that day that they wished they had the confidence to do what we did. I consistently responded to them, "Why can't you?"

It was that day that I realized something very important: everybody is looking for something to take their mind off, even for a brief moment, the troubles of their day.

A friend once told me, "Don't worry about what people think about you because they don't think about you." What a sobering statement! But damn—how true! We spend countless hours worrying about what others think, and the bulk of the time folks are only worried about their own problems. If they are worried about us, it is only to mask their insecurities or to escape their own reality for a short moment.

When I finally worked up the courage to put on that catsuit with John, I realized that our silliness was actually helping others. It was helping them forget about their troubles for a brief moment and laugh. The whole thing was a tremendous social experiment of what can potentially happen when you get out of your own head. As our catsuit adventures continued in the days, months, and years to follow, we crossed paths with many people who needed a reminder of the joy in life. Our role in helping others and our purpose in life was solidified. In addition, we identified one of our favorite FUNdamentals—dressing up in costume for no good reason!

FUN Chapter Takeaways

- Don't dwell on the past. Focus on what you can influence—the future. This is called "forward-thinking."

- Mirror what positive people do, so you too will experience that same positivity.

- Identify your FUNdamentals and seek them out regularly, especially when you feel discouraged or down.

- Get creative in identifying your FUNdamentals. Even something as outlandish as prancing around in a catsuit can provide you and others unexpected and honest delight!

Next Up

Now that I've given you some examples of how I incorporate fundamism in my life, we'll explore how to find yours. Where can you start in finding your own FUNdamentals? What may be holding you back in creating more FUN in your life?

In the next chapter, we'll explore your personal foundation and what makes you experience life the way you currently do. In doing so, you put yourself in a more advantageous position to identify your FUNdamentals and begin incorporating them into your life every day.

Chapter 3
The Foundation of F.U.N.

"You cannot **build a dream** on a foundation of sand. To weather the test of storms, it must be **cemented in the heart** with uncompromising conviction."

—*T.F. Hodge*

At the age of thirty-three, I was an executive director of operations for a Fortune 300 company. My first day in the role I remember crossing paths with one of our employees. We made eye contact; we had never met before. They didn't know who I was, and it didn't matter. I smiled and greeted them with a boisterous, "Great morning!" No response and confusion set in.

How could anyone make eye contact, be asked a direct question, and just keep walking after completely ignoring me?

Over the years the above experience has happened to me numerous times. Even to this day, the lack of human response after a warm greeting still catches me off guard, and I find myself wondering why.

A speaker by the name of Keith Harrell used to recite a quote by his grandmother that really stuck with me. She used to tell him, "Don't ever judge the face if you can't judge the heart. You never know where someone has been in life, and you don't know what they are going through. Growing up, your grandma gave you so many smiles, so if someone doesn't have one, bless them with one of your own." I don't know why some individuals look at me, see my smile, hear my happy greeting, and choose not to reply. However, the one thing I know for certain is that that individual could benefit from having a little more F.U.N. in life.

As already mentioned in the introduction, F.U.N. is an acronym that stands for *foundation, understanding others' perspectives,* and identifying *next steps.* It is predicated on your being present and willing to consistently indulge in self-reflection. F.U.N. represents a balance of recognizing strengths, areas of opportunity, personal awareness, respect of others, curiosity, and willingness to move yourself forward.

In chapters 1, 2, and currently in 3, we've been examining the *foundation* of fundamism, the F in F.U.N. A key part of this foundation entails a whole-hearted embrace of the notion that you choose your perspective on life (chapter 1). You choose to take on the victim or victor mindset. A second key is that you identify your FUNdamentals and engage in them frequently to keep alit your life lantern of joy, and satisfaction (chapter 2). In this chapter we'll explore other crucial components in the foundation of F.U.N., starting with being present in life and deliberate in our actions. These two behaviors are critical in maximizing the effectiveness of F.U.N.

Presence

The Oxford Dictionary defines the word "present" as being "fully focused on or involved in what one is doing or experiencing." Oftentimes I find myself in a situation where I'm physically present but not mentally there. You could say I'm not "fully focused." In order to truly get the most out of every day and experience the delight of life as it unfolds in real time, we must be present. Sure, I struggle with this, as so many of us do.

For example, if you're currently reading this in a setting where others are around you, take a look and count how many individuals are on some form of device. Cell phones, computers, tablets, and other technology have made life a lot easier in many regards. However, they've completely destroyed our ability to communicate with one another without interruption or be 100% present in most situations.

If fundamism, i.e., having more FUN in life, is something you know you could benefit from and are committed to implementing, I challenge you to set aside some time in every day where you're completely free of technology. Over time, you'll feel a sense of freedom, enjoyment, and presence in these moments. You'll likely end up extending your technology-free time, so you can enjoy that freedom more and more each day.

Deliberate

If you had to rate your ability to be deliberate in the things you do on a scale from 1 to 10, how would you rank yourself? Specifically, how often do you approach your day with a plan? In the space below, place your ranking and list a few of the items you find you approach deliberately on a regular basis. What behaviors or items do you believe you could be more deliberate in doing on a regular basis?

How deliberate are you? (1 being the lowest, 10 being the highest)

What are some items you approach deliberately on a regular basis? (Examples could include: morning rituals, team meetings, workouts, shopping for specific items, etc.)

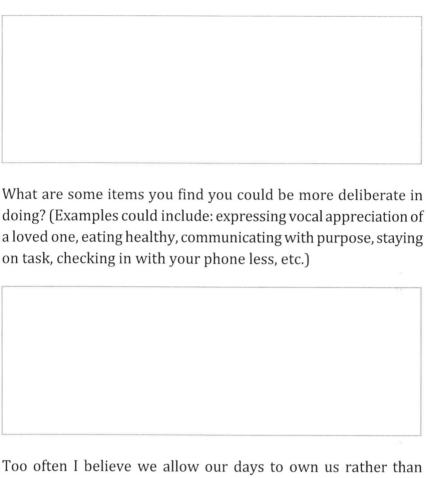

What are some items you find you could be more deliberate in doing? (Examples could include: expressing vocal appreciation of a loved one, eating healthy, communicating with purpose, staying on task, checking in with your phone less, etc.)

Too often I believe we allow our days to own us rather than owning the day. As prisoners of the moment, we get sucked into things that we believe to be important and fall victim to distractions. When was the last time you came into work with specific things you wanted to accomplish, began the tasks, were notified of a new email, and you were off doing something else?

Being deliberate in your day means that you have to place a priority on the things you want to achieve and devote resources to ensure they happen. Attack each day with purpose and watch your productivity improve exponentially.

As you begin to set goals and deliberately take the steps necessary to complete them, fulfillment in life both personally and professionally will follow in abundance. And as you already probably know, it is fun to feel fulfilled. Fun and fulfillment are the aims of fundamism.

Are you ready for some FUN? Are you completely present and reading this in an environment devoid of distraction? Are you being deliberate, open, and honest with yourself about what you hope to receive by educating yourself on fundamism? If so, let's take a deeper dive into the F—*foundation*—of fundamism. Let's look at how experience plays a role in the foundation of F.U.N.

Experience

People who love life and appear to be consistently upbeat are not impervious to despair or heartache. As an international speaker, I travel all over the world for workshops and keynote addresses. I typically ask individuals attending my sessions to raise their hands if they grew up in a single-parent household. I follow that be saying raise or keep your hand raised if you grew up in what you consider poverty. Raise or keep your hand raised if you have known or know someone who has been affected by cancer. Finally I add, raise or keep your hand raised if you've experienced the loss of someone close to you. Very few of my audience members have ever not raised a hand to one of those questions. What does that mean? Everyone on this Earth is faced with challenges, disappointment, and setbacks. These difficult experiences help make us who we are, shape much of our life perspective, and help establish our foundation.

Our experiences in life help mold our belief system. This belief system drives much of our behavior. Ultimately, our behavior is a key factor in the creation of our emotions.

Take, for example, my brother, Chris. I mentioned earlier many of the challenging characteristics my father displayed on a regular basis. These characteristics coupled with many other factors negatively impacted the relationship between him and Chris. I recall them having many arguments, which was a driving factor in my brother's decision to move out of the house his sophomore year of high school. These tough experiences helped shape Chris's belief system.

I don't know where you all stand on the nature vs. nurture debate, but I'm certain we are a product of both. DNA absolutely plays a role in our personality, actions, and ability. Educating yourself, gravitating towards the things that give you strength, and surrounding yourself with amazing people can play a huge role in these things, as well.

I remember Chris telling me on multiple occasions that he got all of our dad's least desirable traits and I got all of his great ones. This, of course, could not be further from the truth. My brother is FANTASTIC! He's great with people, extremely skilled, and has a huge heart. Despite the fact that everyone he meets feels his impact, his formative experiences with our father shaped his belief system into thinking something different. It is Chris's belief that his destiny was shaped by our father. This belief drives his behaviors and too often, his emotions. His lack of hope and optimism have been debilitating at times. I asked him once why he always had to think the worst in things. His response: "So I'm not disappointed later."

The interesting thing about Chris's journey and perspective is that I agree with him. I do think that his destiny was shaped by our father, just as mine was too. What we disagree on is how it's been shaped. Chris and I were born to the same mother and father. We have similar personality traits. The difference is I began emulating the behaviors of others I wanted to be like and also paid close attention to the undesirable behaviors exhibited by those near me. My father had a ton of positive traits. I learned who I wanted to be by watching both the great and not-so-great in everyone. Rather than feeling I was destined for a difficult life, I felt I was destined to help others see they weren't:

If you don't like your experience in life, change your life experiences!

The point that I'm trying to make is that if you are feeling a lack of happiness or fulfillment, try introducing new and fun experiences to your life. Those experiences will impact your belief system, which will drive your behaviors and generate different emotions.

If you want a different experience in life, you have to experience life differently. Is your job sucking all your energy away, leaving you depressed and anxious about going in every day? Take the steps necessary to change the situation. Do you have a toxic relationship driving unwanted stress or negativity? Approach the relationship differently or do something about it. Tired of feeling sluggish, down about your health, or lacking confidence based on your physical appearance? Make the necessary changes to ensure growth and that will get you in a better mindset.

I've seen a ton of growth in my brother Chris in the last several years. The reason? He started looking more forward than in the rear view (i.e., forward-thinking). He surrounded himself with amazing people who valued him. And, Chris started doing more things that he enjoyed, his FUNdamentals. In short, he introduced new life experiences into his life, which have changed his take on life from glass-half-empty to glass-half-full!

Personality Traits

While much of our foundation can be built through experience, there are additional factors involved. When I use the term, "foundation," I'm referring to everything that makes you, you.

Along with life experiences, personality traits, communication style, purpose, and guiding principles play major roles in our day-to-day experience of life.

Self-reflection and focusing on how to improve the things within our control will have a significant impact in driving different and more positive experiences.

Who is the individual in your life that appears to have the most fun?

Describe some fun memories of this individual or examples where they demonstrated fun.

How can you incorporate some of these examples or behaviors into your life?

Ever wonder why some individuals thrive with structure and others don't? Or why talking to strangers can come so natural to some but not others? Our differences are driven by many things, some referenced in the paragraphs above. However, the most defining difference in individuals is personality style.

Years ago, a gentleman by the name of Richard Stephenson created the DOPE 4 Bird Personality Test. The intent was to assign bird types to the four different personality styles based on the original studies of Dr. Gary Couture. It is not a psychological evaluation but rather an activity rooted in self-assessment to gain a better understanding of yourself and others.

As personality style is a staple in the composition of a person's foundation, recognizing what style you are and how it manifests itself in your environment can provide additional context for why you experience the world the way you do. In addition, it may allow you the insight necessary to improve your quality of life, strength of relationships, self-acceptance, and awareness.

The four DOPE bird styles can be found below. As you read through them, try to identify what bird represents you and those closest to you. A more detailed, comprehensive version of this assessment can be found at richardstep.com. For the purpose of this exercise, we'll keep it simple. It is important to note that you can be represented by more than one bird style. One may just play a more dominant role than the other.

Dove

The dove is a warm, caring, and relationship-driven individual. They enjoy making others feel comfortable and thrive in team environments. Doves love feeling appreciated and will likely make others feel the same. Typically, they listen well, are sympathetic to others, and avoid conflict. Lastly, the dove is super chill and doesn't move at a very rapid pace. You might find doves holding positions such as teachers, guidance counselors, or social workers. If you go out to eat with a dove, they may be the individual asking what everyone else is getting to eat, telling you how delicious that sounds, and asking if you'd like to try their meal. They may even offer to pick up the bill just to get on your good side! Doves can be identified as warm and slow-moving.

Owl

The owl is an individual who thrives in structure and detail. An owl's decision-making process is based heavily on logic and can take more time than others due to an extensive review of details. They are driven by facts far more than emotion or opinion, and aren't known for taking a ton of risk. You can find many owls working as scientists, librarians, accountants, or engineers. If you go out to eat with an owl, they might be the one asking about the specials and trying to identify what meal offers the best value. Logically, it makes sense to pay for our own respective meals, so prepare to have your payment method ready when eating with an owl! Owls can be identified as cold and slow-moving.

Peacock

You all ready to party?! The peacock is the beacon of light in nearly every situation. They are lighthearted, fun, and enjoy being around others. Peacocks are typically creative, optimistic, and overflowing with enthusiasm! Oftentimes, they struggle with structure, expressing impatience, and can be distracted easily. Peacocks can be found holding positions in sales, marketing, and music. If you go out to eat with a peacock, they might be the individual telling all the jokes, carrying the bulk of conversation, and telling the server multiple times that they haven't even looked at the menu yet. No need to pay, the peacock is going to expense this meal! Peacocks can be identified as warm and fast-moving.

Eagle

Looking for a leader? The eagle will carry your squad. Assertive, dominant, and decisive, the eagle is a natural when it comes to leading a team. Like the owl, the eagle thrives in structure and appreciates facts over opinions. They move fast and can be impatient, at times. Without ill intent, the eagle can often be insensitive to the needs of others based on their desire to get things done quickly. If you go out to eat with an eagle, they most likely will be the driving force behind choosing the location and will know what they want to eat before even looking at a menu. As eagles can be found in positions of leadership like CEOs, executives, or other high-ranking officials, you should allow them to pick up the bill. Eagles can be identified as cold and fast-moving.

Which bird style best represents you?

Now think about your family and what drives many of your commonalities or differences. Your personality style plays a critical role in how you see the world. Personalities drive perspective, communication style, how we approach tasks, and the experiences we have in life. Taking the time to understand why you respond the way you do and exploring the nuances of others' personalities will help facilitate change in the areas you seek it most. We'll explore these personality styles a little more in the upcoming chapter "Understanding Others' Perspectives."

Purpose

Thus far we've established that our experiences shape much of who we are and what we do. In addition, we've provided a little insight into how our personalities drive perspective and experience. The thread that ties both of these items together is purpose. Every foundation serves a purpose, to support its attached structure. Therefore, shouldn't we as individuals have purpose? Shouldn't this purpose be a driving force within our foundation and help create the fulfillment we all seek?

Oftentimes, if a person is present enough to have found their true purpose, it manifests itself in all that they do. You can see their purpose in how they interact with others, how they conduct business, how they raise their family, and how they experience life. Their personality supports this purpose. It shines brightly as they go about the activities and interactions of their day.

To show you what I mean, I'll tell you about how purpose manifests across all areas of my life. I believe my purpose is to reveal the opportunity available to us all to have more FUN in life. My foundation is rooted in FUN, and it manifests itself in all that I do.

Recently, I was keynoting a conference for the Wisconsin Bankers Association. I had never met any of the attendees before entering the venue.

My outfit was fire! I had on pink pants, fun socks, a hip shirt, a light blue jacket with a pink pocket square, and a bright patterned bowtie. As I made my way through the conference, I walked confidently as I felt great in this new outfit I had just purchased. My shoulders were back and my head high when a young lady approached me issuing an unbridled excitement.

"You must be Paul!" she exclaimed.

"How did you know that?" I responded.

"My name is Jennifer, and I'll be introducing you today at the conference. I saw your outfit, the way that you carried yourself, and the energy that surrounds you. You are FUN! I knew that you had to be our speaker as I read about your concept of fundamism. You appear to be the most fun person in the room, and I applaud you for living your truth."

Jennifer's quick take on me as well as many similar assessments by others validated to me that my purpose manifests itself in all that I do—in my very being. Compound that with the fact that my five-year-old daughter, Adalyn Grace, describes me as fun, silly, and kind, and I'm certain my purpose reveals itself in my personality.

There are many different purposes in life. Some desire to be the best father or mother who raise children to be kind and respectful of others. Some feel their purpose is to create things of value. Others are driven by improving some aspect of society and find purpose in moving humanity forward.

Your purpose is exactly that, YOURS. No one can define your purpose for you. It takes self-reflection and dedication in its identification. Some are born with purpose. Others find it in their journey of life. Many of those reading this haven't found their true purpose, and that's perfectly acceptable. What's not acceptable and detrimental to the success of you living a life of fun and fulfillment is if you never spend time identifying your purpose.

Below are a series of questions crucial in helping you articulate your foundation. Take some time to reflect and jot down your answers below or on a separate piece of paper. If you don't have the answers now, know that you've identified the first step necessary in experiencing F.U.N., so give it some time and thought, and return again later.

If you'd consider yourself purpose-driven, what is your purpose? (Don't get too hung up on this if it doesn't come to you. We'll work together later in chapter 5, Next Steps to Create More F.U.N., to help narrow your focus and identify your true purpose.)

How does your purpose manifest itself in the work setting?

If the people with whom you work were to describe you in three words, what three words would they choose?

How does your purpose manifest itself at home?

If your family or friends were to describe you in three words, what three words would they choose?

_____

With the purpose you outlined above in mind and using only three words, how would you want ALL those with whom you interact to describe you?

_____

In theory, if you live life with purpose it should manifest itself in all that you do. The words that people use to describe you would be consistent with how you'd describe yourself and align directly with the purpose you serve. This isn't something that typically happens overnight. You have to be patient with yourself in your journey. We're all a work in progress.

Taking the time to identify where you are in that process and what you're willing to do to move forward will help you find fundamism in your life. Most importantly, it will lay the groundwork in ensuring your foundation supports all the FUN you desire (or can handle)!

Not only is self-reflection pivotal in generating growth and maximizing FUN, it is one of our core FUNdamentals.

By learning more about how your experiences help shape you, the role your personality plays in life, and identifying a purpose that drives you, you can begin to determine what aspects of your foundation are the strongest and where you may need a little work.

FUN Chapter Takeaways

- When you avoid distractions like daydreaming or playing with your phone and instead you are present in the moment, you best position yourself to experience delight and satisfaction.

- When you are deliberate with your time and resources, you end up being more productive, thus more fulfilled.

- To flip the script on any feelings of sadness, boredom, or frustration that may haunt you, introduce new experiences into your life.

- Take the time to understand your personality as well as the nuances of others' personalities. In doing so, you'll be better equipped to deal with challenging situations and to create more FUN in your interactions with others.

- Determine your purpose. When you are able to pursue your purpose in your work and personal life, then you will feel great joy and fulfillment.

Next Up

Your foundation plays a crucial role in creating a life of contentment and fun. However, it is only one element of F.U.N. Self-improvement comes not only through self-reflection and self-development but in making the effort to understand others' perspectives.

Making deeper connections with others is the next chapter's focus. By genuinely seeking to an understanding of others' perspectives, you can avoid negative interactions, drive more memorable experiences in life, and attract more FUN!

Chapter 4
The F.U.N. in Understanding Others' Perspectives

"I don't like that man. **I must get to know him better.**"

—*Abraham Lincoln*

Now that our foundation is in place and we're taking steps to maximize its effectiveness, we can move to the U in F.U.N.: *understanding others' perspectives.*

Just as experience drives much of our individual belief system, behaviors, and emotions, it has the same effect on others. Showing a genuine interest in learning about the background, upbringing, ideas, and concerns of those around you can provide you more insight into their perspective. Having a better understanding of how another person sees the world may allow you a more comprehensive view of what drives the differences between you and them. In doing so, you might be surprised at the meaningful, trusting, and sustainable relationship that results. Family, friends, coworkers, and customers will all respect and appreciate you more. Most importantly, you and everyone around you will experience a greater sense of fun.

Does this sound too good to be true? It did to me at one point in my life, as well. It wasn't until I learned how to drive these types of relationships and experience them firsthand, that I finally bought in.

The Open Mind

A fellow speaker and good friend of mine by the name of Adam Carroll told me once that there are two ways to approach any person or situation. These two ways will dictate how you experience life and will play a major role in creating outcomes. When approaching any person or situation, you can decide to be:

1. *Curious*

2. *Furious*

Have you ever been in a work setting and found yourself observing the actions or attitudes of others? Maybe you were watching one specific individual in a meeting and felt they were being condescending. Or perhaps you received an email from someone and thought to yourself, "What crawled up this person's rear end?" Whatever the situation, you have two ways to approach it. You can be *curious* or *furious*.

Curious individuals look at someone else's behavior and ask what could be driving it. This curiosity may create questions like: Why is this person acting this way? What happened in this individual's life to generate this behavior? Who does this individual have in their life to turn to when things get rough? What can I do to potentially make this individual's day just a little better? A truly self-reflective and honest individual might even ask what behavior they themselves are demonstrating that could be driving the behavior of others around them. Those that are curious do what is within their control to try and get others to their level rather than dropping down to the level of others.

Furious individuals look at someone's behavior and make judgments. They allow others' behaviors to drive irritation and resentment. Individuals who approach things from a *furious* perspective might make fun of those that are different, exude anger towards them, or let the attitudes of others negatively impact their day.

Understanding others' perspectives takes patience and an open mind. The following quote was taken from "Hsin-Hsin Ming" written by Seng-Ts'an, the Third Zen Patriarch of China:

If you wish to see the truth, hold no opinion for or against anything.

Behavior is so multifaceted and multidimensional that it would be a mistake to believe you know why someone acts the way they do based on a small sample size of interactions. I believe what Seng-Ts'an was saying was that our preconceived ideas of things (in this case, of others) can impact our ability to experience them as they were meant to be. Some call this the self-fulfilling prophecy as your perception or judgments can create a false sense of reality and drive the outcome you have in your mind. To truly understand others' perspectives, you have to approach your interactions with an open mind and with "no opinion for or against anything." In turn, you're more likely to experience greater satisfaction.

Genuine Interest

Now that we've established the importance of limiting judgments in regard to other people and situations, let's take an even deeper dive into understanding the perspective of others. In doing so, you'll have greater access to FUN over frustration, and you might establish stronger relationships as a result.

Whether at work, a networking event, a class reunion, or any situation where you could be having discussions with others, what are some of the most consistent topics that come up in conversation? In my experience, I can count on three coming up; work, family, and weather. The questions I hear regularly when out and about are, "What do you do for a living?" "How long have you been married?" Do you have children?" and "How's the weather back home?"

The most crucial aspect of understanding others' perspectives is showing a genuine interest in them. How often do you meet someone who appears sincere in their interest of you? The truth of the matter is, the bulk of folks are too busy talking about themselves or asking the same questions as everyone else. As a result, meaningful connections aren't created as regularly as they could be. The result—we're missing out on even more FUN.

In the summer of 2017, I recall being on a flight to Dallas. I selected my usual window seat, hoping that the middle would be left open. I had my headphones in bumping "King of Wishful Thinking" by Steve Winwood when an elderly woman settled in right next to me. She placed her bag under the seat but that wasn't the only baggage she was carrying. When I boarded the plane, I had a plan of keeping to myself. When I began to FEEL her strife through the energy she was emitting, I had to engage.

"Are you flying home or headed someplace fun?" I asked.

She replied, "I was in Kansas City for my brother's funeral."

"My goodness, I'm sorry to hear of his passing. How many siblings do you have?" I continued.

"Just the one," she answered, appearing more troubled with every question I asked.

I kept on with the same theme oblivious to the painful environment I was complicit in sustaining. "When was the last time you saw each other?"

"That's what makes it so hard," she responded. "We haven't seen each other for years, and I feel terrible for not visiting sooner."

I realized I was digging myself a hole. Every question I asked forced her to be reminded of the very thing that was giving her heartache. My goal was to help lift her up but without having taken a deliberate approach to the questions I was asking, I was failing miserably. If I was going to help change her mindset and get her out of this rut (at least temporarily), I had to switch up my game plan.

"Tell me about a time when you and your brother were the closest, when you had the most FUN together," I asked.

Her disposition began to change, and she gave a little smirk. "When we were kids, we didn't have a care in the world. We'd dance and act up without any fear of what others thought. We'd play for hours on end. Those were the good ole' days," she said.

Finally I asked her the million-dollar question, "What's your name?"

"Phyllis," she responded.

"Phyllis, what's something you're super proud of that not many people know about you?"

She lit up with a smile that could brighten any room! "When my first husband passed, I was in my early fifties and had never had a job," she stated. "I put myself through college and got a job as a manager at an engineering firm."

Phyllis and I continued our conversation for the remainder of the flight talking about what we do for fun now, the most significant leaders in our life, and other interesting stories. For a brief moment, Phyllis wasn't thinking about the passing of her brother.

She was consumed by one of the most powerful FUNdamentals in existence, showing a genuine interest in others, and was forced to think about things that gave her strength.

We all have the power to make a difference in someone else's day. By asking questions that force people to think, individuals are forced to be present in conversation. Being present allows you to experience life to the fullest, without judgment or distraction. It allows you the opportunity to move past your troubles while bringing more joy and fulfillment to the moment. This doesn't typically happen when asking the same old questions about work, family, or the weather.

Below are some examples of questions that you could ask friends, family, coworkers or customers that might spark a more fruitful conversation, which in turn should result in greater fun and satisfaction for both parties. What questions might you add?

- What is something you're proud of that not many people know about you?

- Tell me about your favorite vacation.

- What would you consider your greatest accomplishment in life thus far?

- Who is somebody in your life that you really look up to?

- We are 70 years young sipping piña coladas on the beach and talking through the legacies that we left. How do you want yours to look?

- What is the worst job you ever had?

- What is the last thing you can recall that made you laugh out loud?

- If you could tell me the most valuable lesson you've learned in the last several years, what would it be?

- What do you do for fun?

- If you absolutely had to do karaoke, what song would you choose?

- If someone close were to describe your personality in three words, what words would they choose?

- Tell me about your favorite hobbies.

- What is the funniest thing that's ever happened to you?

- What was the first concert you attended?

- What is a project that you're working on currently that you really enjoy?

- Who was your favorite celebrity hero or crush growing up?

If you're struggling to come up with fresh, thought-provoking conversation and need a little help, it might benefit to learn more about noticing and connecting questions.

Noticing questions are based off of things that you observe. For example, you might see an interesting item on a coworker's desk. Leveraging that observation you may ask, "I noticed that cool little trinket on your desk with a quote on it. What's it say?" Another example could pertain to something an individual is wearing. For example, "I noticed you wear bow-ties regularly and I really like them. How many would you say you have?" Typically when you ask about things that interest others, they will be far more willing to engage and appreciate you for taking the time to ask. In doing so, individuals might consider the situation, and even you, more FUN!

Connecting questions are based off of like interests. These questions help form connections and can help build trust. For example, you might spark a conversation by asking about a mutual friend, "I saw that you and I have several mutual connections on LinkedIn. How do you know Bob Smith?" Hobbies, sports, entertainment, restaurants, and education are all additional topics that could help provide a connection between two parties. Another example could sound something like, "Did I see you and your family over at that Italian restaurant off of 5th last week? We've been going there for years. What did you order?"

There are a number of different ways and techniques that could drive more meaningful interactions with others. Whether you use noticing, connecting, or any other type of question, the goal is to show a genuine interest. In doing so, you'll provide a FUN experience to those with whom you connect while building stronger, trust-based, sustainable relationships with them.

Articulated Expectations and Motivations

The next step in understanding others' perspectives is taking time to recognize their expectations and motivations. Have you ever been frustrated by someone for not doing something that you never told them to do? How could someone possibly fulfill the expectations you have of them if they don't even know what they are? Conversely, how could you know how to fulfill someone else's expectations of you if you never took the time to ask what they were?

Uncommunicated expectations cause preplanned resentments.

Taking the time to communicate expectations can go a long way in building relationships. Wouldn't it be a lot easier to connect with others if we asked them what they wanted from the relationship and how we currently stack up? Brutally honest feedback can scare some. However, there is a small faction of people that appreciate real feedback because it gives them the opportunity to improve.

What could potentially happen if you asked one of your customers to rank your business relationship on a scale from 1 to 10? Preface the question with the fact that you pride yourself in differentiating the service you provide through the client relationships you share and are always looking for ways to maximize your value offering. That kind of preface along with the question could go a long way in building trust. If you go this route, you must be prepared for whatever assessment they give you. Remember that their number is based solely off the expectations they have of the relationship. Therefore, the perfect follow-up question to gain a better understanding of what they expect could be, "How do I get to a 10?" Clarifying expectations allows you a higher probability in fulfilling them. What individual doesn't find delight in making others happy?

While there are many other contributing factors in understanding others' perspectives, the final piece we'll be covering in this chapter is the different ways in which individuals are motivated. As discussed in the previous chapter, The Foundation of F.U.N., personality styles play a huge role in all that we do. Educating yourself on the different bird styles in the DOPE 4 Bird Personality Test could go a long way in providing insight into how to communicate with others and better understand what motivates them.

In the spirit of simplification, we'll only be exploring the two main types of motivators, *intrinsic* motivation and *extrinsic* motivation. Intrinsic motivators come from within. Individuals motivated intrinsically want to do a good job because it creates a sense of personal achievement. In contrast, extrinsic motivators come from outside sources. Individuals motivated extrinsically are likely to complete a task or behavior to receive a reward or to avoid being punished. Rewards can be tangible items, verbal recognition from others, or even a high score.

Below are two individuals who work for a pharmaceutical firm. We will use their profiles to show how an inability to adapt to different personality styles and motivation can manifest itself in the work setting.

- Joanne Burch works as a pharmaceutical sales rep and is a dominant peacock. Her secondary bird style is the dove, and she loves to make others laugh while placing significant value in relationships. Joanne is motivated extrinsically and loves to be told she's doing a great job. She has many sales awards and takes pride in being the top dog.

- Joanne reports directly to Dave Franklin. Dave is a dominant eagle with owl tendencies. He strives for excellence to fulfill the expectations that he places on himself and is intrinsically motivated. Dave is not vocal in his appreciation of others as he feels they're just doing what they were hired to do. However, he does pay close attention to the sales numbers and recognizes that some individuals are more skilled than others.

I'm sure you can see where this is going. To thrive in communication and build more quality relationships, it is our responsibility to adapt our style to meet that of those with whom we interact. It's easy for us to communicate to others in a manner that's most convenient to us. However, our style doesn't always resonate with folks who have a different personality or are motivated by other things.

Most people are so interested in their own stories that it seems silly to invite them into your own, a place they have no interest in playing a part. Knowing this and modifying your style to meet them where they are will make a world of difference in creating more meaningful connections with others. Having stronger relationships in life will reduce the number of challenging situations in which you find yourself and improve the likelihood of everyone having more FUN!

If Dave doesn't express vocal appreciation for the work Joanne is doing, she will grow frustrated, and burnout could potentially take place. As a result, Joanne won't have as much fun, and the pharmaceutical firm could lose one of its top salespeople due to a lack of communication. On the opposite end of the spectrum, if Joanne is consistently looking to be rewarded for achievements that fall under the basic requirements of the job, Dave could begin to resent her, have less fun in his role, and look to minimize their number of interactions.

Now let's explore two individuals that live under the same roof. We will use their profiles to show how an inability to adapt to different personality styles and motivation can manifest itself at home.

- Holly Swanson works as a statistics professor for a prominent state university. She loves data and identifies as an owl. Holly is extremely smart and uses facts to support her arguments. When hanging with the family, Holly prefers to stay in and enjoy quiet time together. Her perfect evening would be ordering a pizza and hanging together in the family room while everyone reads or does crossword puzzles independently.

- Holly is married to Rich Swanson. Rich is a stay-at-home dad who lives to help others. If you were to look up images of a dove in Google, Rich's picture would be the first to come up. Rich leverages emotion and feelings a lot in conversation and just wants Holly to appreciate him for all the love he gives to the family. His ideal night would be making a delicious dinner for the family and allowing each member to identify one game they want to play together. Everyone gets a turn, and everyone goes to bed happy!

As you can see, we have two vastly different personalities joined in wedlock. Some say opposites attract and having differences can be healthy for a relationship. In order for Holly and Rich to live in harmony, they must exercise compromise and proper communication. Holly is an introvert by nature who isn't vocal in expressing her feelings. She must adapt to Rich's style when necessary. On the flip side, Rich loves making others happy, but Holly isn't outwardly expressive. It's Rich's duty to adapt to Holly when necessary and understand that she doesn't love in the same manner as he loves. If compromise isn't made and both parties don't exercise flexibility, the ability to have fun together is significantly impacted.

The key to successful communication and overall satisfaction and harmony is balancing the needs of all those involved. Meeting individuals where they are, setting proper expectations with all parties, and understanding the differences in individual motivators will help maximize your overall effectiveness in driving the types of meaningful relationships you seek. As a result, you'll be connected to others in a deeper manner thus reducing the number of negative interactions and increasing the opportunity for more fun in life.

At the end of the day every person is motivated by experience.

Do you know someone who appears to be motivated by money? What does money buy? *Experience.* Who can you identify that is motivated by title, promotion, or power? What does being a boss allow you to do? Drive *experience.* Can you remember someone in your life that appeared to be motivated by vocal appreciation? What could that be driven by? The *experience* of feeling valued! If you create an experience that shows others they are important and that you genuinely care about them, you might experience better relationships as a result. When you have better relationships, you notice a sense of fulfillment and joy in regard to your life in general. It's powerful!

Having an unbiased perspective of others' personalities can help create relationships characterized by trust, respect, love, and fun. Doves, owls, peacocks, and eagles can thrive together so long as all parties are willing to be flexible. Crossing quadrants into other bird styles is where conflict can take place. Understanding how each personality works, feels, responds, and plays can minimize potential conflict and replace it with mutual admiration, which increases everyone's fun.

There's a lot that goes into understanding others' perspectives. Realizing that our experiences help drive the differences between us and allowing yourself to be *curious* rather than *furious* can help you avoid ill-placed judgment. In addition, showing a genuine interest in others by asking questions that truly matter can make a world of difference in driving more fun interactions. Taking into account all of these things while recognizing differences in personalities and personal motivations will provide a well-rounded approach to understanding others. That, of course, will allow you to be one step closer to maximizing FUN!

FUN Chapter Takeaways

- Keeping an open mind and being more curious than furious can reduce your number of negative experiences and instill a positive frame of mind.

- Expressing a genuine interest in others and asking meaningful questions can drive stronger connections, thus upping the fun quotient.

- Taking the time to learn others' expectations increases your probability of meeting them, thus increasing your overall number of positive interactions.

- At the end of the day, everyone is motivated by experience. Take the time to create a fun, impactful experience for others and watch everyone's level of delight skyrocket!

Next Up

We've examined your personal foundation and explored how understanding others' perspectives can create more overall fun. It's now time to introduce the N in F.U.N., with N being "next steps."

The coming chapter offers a series of specific tactical exercises to help you have more FUN in your life. This will be where you put many of the principles discussed in previous chapters into practice and drive significant behavioral change to bring on the good times in all you do!

Chapter 5
Next Steps to Even More F.U.N.

"It was **character** that got us out of bed, **commitment** that moved us into **action**, and **discipline** that enabled us to follow through."

—Zig Ziglar

Congratulations! You've made it through some self-reflection in your foundation and have taken some time to understand others' perspectives. Now we can begin building your personal implementation strategy and move on to the N in F.U.N. because without it, it's just F.U.! Welcome to *next steps*.

This is not a traditional book chapter. Creating your own personal implementation strategy to incorporate fundamism and have more FUN in life is dependent on you engaging in some self-discovery. Figuring out next steps is your journey, and I can only be a guide along the way. As such, this chapter is filled with activities that lead you through your unique path to fulfillment. They will lay the groundwork for your personal and deliberate approach to contentment.

The following next-step activities will allow you to identify what drives you and where you go from here. They are structured in the same order as the concepts introduced in chapters 3 and 4 on your foundation and understanding others' perspectives. Move at a pace in which you are comfortable. These activities should provide insight and will only work when you devote yourself to doing them right, not just doing them to check them off a timeline you arbitrarily created. This is your opportunity to be 100% honest and transparent. Take your time, enjoy every step, and be as thorough as possible. Your ability to connect to your life through FUN depends on it!

Foundation

Experience

As discussed in chapter 3, The Foundation of F.U.N., your experiences in life help establish your belief system. Your belief system plays a huge role in driving your behavior, and this behavior significantly impacts your emotions. If you are interested in experiencing life a little differently, then you have to introduce new experiences in life. To determine what experiences will maximize FUN for you, you have to take some time reflecting on how your perspective was created. This will allow you a better understanding in what's been holding you back from living a life of joy and contentment, it will provide you a greater chance of moving forward in achieving growth.

The following experience activities are based on self-reflection. They require you to dig deep into your memory bank to answer the questions that identify why you experience life the way you do. Some of these memories may be joyous, others painful. It is crucial that you are vulnerable in the process to ensure the growth you seek.

1. **Background**—The following questions help identify the moments and people in your life that helped shape your perspective.

What experiences stand out as the most profound in creating your philosophy of living or "perspective" on life?

Specifically, what experiences in your life have driven the way you see yourself, those around you, and your typical take on daily experiences?

Examples could be but aren't limited to:

Divorce, loss of a loved one, moving a lot, an eating disorder, abuse, moments of exhilaration, time with loved ones, vacations, presence or lack thereof of family or a spiritual community.

How did these experiences shape your perspective on life?

What were some negative outcomes in your life that happened as a direct result of the perspective shaped by the experiences listed above?

What were some positive outcomes in your life that happened as a direct result of the perspective shaped by the experiences listed above?

What's the most embarrassing thing that has ever happened to you?

Name a couple that models a loving relationship:

_____

What is it about this relationship you appreciate?

_____

How can the positive elements of this relationship be replicated in your relationships?

What responsibility do you take in the creation of your perspective?

Specifically, without blaming other people or situations for how you see things, what role did YOU play in creating your perspective?

What could you do TODAY that would allow you to take more responsibility of your perspective from now moving forward?

[blank response box]

Name a situation that's happened in the last month where you went negative. What could a positive interpretation of that experience be?

[blank response box]

2. **Intentionally or Unintentionally**—We either live our lives intentionally or unintentionally, and our overall experience in life is greatly impacted by this. Individuals that live intentionally typically have more F.U.N. and fulfillment in life. This is a direct result of being more present and having greater success in achieving the goals they set for themselves. This activity will help identify how deliberate you are in your actions and what steps to take to live a more intentional life.

Your morning sets the tone for how the rest of your day may go. List the five things you do intentionally when you wake up in the morning:

1. ....

2. ....

3. ....

4. ....

5. ....

What are some things you could do intentionally in the morning to help drive a different result in how you experience your day?

Examples could include but aren't limited to:

Take thirty seconds to think about what you are thankful for, avoid looking at your cell phone for the first thirty minutes of your day, compliment a loved one, exercise, or write a positive affirmation for the day.

List the five things you do intentionally when you get to work.

1. _____

2. _____

3. _____

4. _____

5. _____

What are some things you could do intentionally at work to help drive a different result in how you experience it?

Examples could include but aren't limited to:

Write a thank-you note to a coworker or customer, write a goal for the day, make yourself laugh, or set aside a block of time to check email and avoid checking it outside of that timeframe.

List the five things you do intentionally when you get home in the evening.

1. _____

2. _____

3. _____

4. _____

5. _____

What are some things you could do intentionally in the evening to help drive a different result in how you experience life at home?

Examples could include but aren't limited to:

Eat dinner together at the table with your family, spouse, or housemates, have everyone in your household share the best things that have happened to them throughout the day, listen to your favorite music, play something creative or imaginary with your kids, or sit outside and talk to loved ones while avoiding technology.

List the five things you do intentionally before you go to bed.

1. _____

2. _____

3. _____

4. _____

5. _____

What are some things you could do intentionally before bed to drive a different result in how you relax or rest?

Examples could be but aren't limited to: self-reflect on the events of the day, identify things that went well, identify things you'd like to improve upon, scratch a loved one's back, or watch your favorite show while being mindless.

3. **Altering Experience**—Taking the time to recognize what is driving negativity in your life and how your behaviors contribute to it can work wonders in driving change. The following activity can help shed some light on what is giving you grief and what to do to mitigate the sting.

What is one aspect of your life that you feel brings stress?

_____

What behaviors or thoughts are you demonstrating that could be driving this negative outcome?

Examples could include but aren't limited to: a lack of money is bringing stress, and the absence of a budget or chaotic spending habits are compounding the issue; your children aren't listening or following directions, and your lack of follow-through in discipline and accountability is making the issue worse; or you have a coworker that you just can't get along with and have never taken the time to learn more about their perspective.

What is one thing that you can do TODAY that could potentially mitigate the stressor you outlined above? (What behavior could you change or incorporate to drive a different outcome?)

Examples could include but aren't limited to: identify a specific time in the day to free yourself of technology or be more deliberate in establishing a routine or budget.

_____

What is another aspect of your life that you feel brings stress?

What behaviors or thoughts are you demonstrating that could be driving this negative outcome?

Examples can be found above.

What is one thing that you can do TODAY that could potentially decrease or remove the stressor you outlined above? (What behavior could you change or incorporate to drive a different outcome?)

Examples could include but aren't limited to: journal throughout the day and identify the best things that have happened to you; or think about how your bird style may have played a role in how you experienced a situation and use that to make a change.

What is one more aspect of your life that you feel brings stress?

What behaviors or thoughts are you demonstrating that could be driving this negative outcome?

Examples could be found above.

What is one thing that you can do TODAY that could potentially mitigate the stressor you outlined above? (What behavior could you change or incorporate to drive a different outcome?)

Examples could include but aren't limited to: jot down all the old experiences in your life keeping you from moving forward and burn or rip the paper up; or give yourself permission to remove these things from your life and do something symbolic to release them.

4. **Your Purpose**—Why are you here? What is your purpose? These are questions many struggle to answer. It's easy to get lost in the activity of our lives, putting things on cruise control and losing sight of the monumental impact we play in creating desired outcomes.

You have more control over your life and surroundings than you could ever imagine. Harnessing this control is easier when you identify your true purpose and align that purpose with all you do. The reason? There's continuity in your actions, which allows you and others a comfort in knowing what to expect. By having purpose and alignment to it, you can access greater fulfillment.

A relationship expert once told me the reason couples break up is they stop living in alignment with their own personal values or purpose. In effect, he said, they forget who they are or desire to be and instead are living according to the values set of the other person. Far too often, he added, the values were never defined and the relationship was on an autopilot course for disaster.

By narrowing down the five core elements of your values set, you can begin to solidify your foundation and help identify your true purpose.

Scan the lists below and circle the words that aptly describe your values. Try to keep the list between 10-15 on the first pass.

The next step will be revealed on the next pages.

Abundance	Boldness	Cooperation	Efficiency
Acceptance	Bravery	Cordiality	Ecstasy
Accessibility	Brilliance	Correctness	Elation
Accomplishment	Buoyancy	Country	Elegance
Acknowledgment	Calmness	Courage	Empathy
Activeness	Camaraderie	Courtesy	Encouragement
Adaptability	Candor	Craftiness	Endurance
Adoration	Capability	Creativity	Energy
Adroitness	Care	Cunning	Enjoyment
Advancement	Carefulness	Curiosity	Entertainment
Adventure	Celebrity	Competitiveness	Enthusiasm
Affection	Certainty	Continuous Improvement	Environmentalism
Affluence	Challenge	Daring	Ethics
Aggressiveness	Change	Decisiveness	Euphoria
Agility	Charity	Decorum	Excellence
Alertness	Chastity	Deference	Excitement
Altruism	Clarity	Delight	Exhilaration
Amazement	Cleanliness	Dependability	Expectancy
Ambition	Clear-mindedness	Depth	Expediency
Amusement	Cleverness	Desire	Experience
Anticipation	Closeness	Determination	Expertise
Appreciation	Comfort	Devotion	Exploration
Approachability	Commitment	Devoutness	Expressiveness
Approval	Community	Dignity	Extravagance
Art	Compassion	Diligence	Extroversion
Articulacy	Competence	Direction	Exuberance
Artistry	Completion	Directness	Equality
Assertiveness	Composure	Discipline	Fairness
Assurance	Concentration	Discovery	Faith
Attentiveness	Confidence	Discretion	Fame
Attractiveness	Conformity	Diversity	Family
Availability	Congruency	Dominance	Fascination
Awareness	Connection	Dreaming	Fashion
Awe	Consciousness	Drive	Fearlessness
Accountability	Conservation	Duty	Ferocity
Accuracy	Consistency	Dynamism	Fidelity
Achievement	Contentment	Decisiveness	Fierceness
Balance	Continuity	Democraticness	Financial
Beauty	Contribution	Eagerness	Firmness
Being the best	Control	Ease	Fitness
Belonging	Conviction	Economy	Flexibility
Benevolence	Conviviality	Education	Flow
Bliss	Coolness	Effectiveness	Fluency

Focus	Industry	Meaning	Prosperity
Fortitude	Influence	Meekness	Prudence
Frankness	Ingenuity	Mindfulness	Purity
Freedom	Insightfulness	Modesty	Patriotism
Friendliness	Inspiration	Motivation	Presence
Friendship	Integrity	Mysteriousness	Pride
Frugality	Intellect	Merit	Proactivity
Fun-Fairness	Intelligence	Mellowness	Professionalism
Family-orientedness	Intensity	Meticulousness	Potency
Fun	Intimacy	Nature	Power
Independence	Intrepidness	Neatness	Practicality
Gallantry	Introspection	Nerve	Pragmatism
	Introversion	Nonconformity	Precision
Gentility	Intuition	Obedience	Preparedness
Giving	Intuitiveness	Open-mindedness	Quality-orientation
Grace	Inventiveness	Openness	Reliability
Gratitude	Investing	Optimism	Resourcefulness
Gregariousness	Involvement	Order	Restraint
Growth	Inner harmony	Organization	Results-oriented
Guidance	Inquisitiveness	Originality	Rationality
Generosity	Intellectual status	Outdoors	Realism
Goodness	Joy	Outlandishness	Reason
	Judiciousness	Outrageousness	Reasonableness
Happiness	Justice	Partnership	Recognition
Harmony	Keenness	Patience	Recreation
Health	Kindness	Passion	Refinement
Heart	Knowledge	Peace	Reflection
Helpfulness	Learning	Perceptiveness	Relaxation
Heroism	Liberation	Perfection	Reliability
Holiness	Liberty	Perkiness	Relief
Honesty	Lightness	Perseverance	Religiousness
Honor	Liveliness	Persistence	Reputation
Hopefulness	Logic	Persuasiveness	Resilience
Hospitality	Longevity	Philanthropy	Resolution
Humility	Love	Piety	Resolve
Humor	Loyalty	Playfulness	Resourcefulness
Hygiene	Leadership	Pleasantness	Respect
Hard work	Legacy	Pleasure	Responsibility
Helping society	Majesty	Poise	Rest
Imagination	Making a difference	Polish	Restraint
Impact	Marriage	Popularity	Reverence
Impartiality	Mastery	Privacy	Richness
Individuality	Maturity	Punctuality	Rigor

Sacredness
Sacrifice
Sagacity
Saintliness
Sanguinity
Satisfaction
Security
Science
Self-reliance
Self-respect
Self-control
Selflessness
Sensitivity
Sensuality
Serenity
Service
Sexiness
Sexuality
Sharing
Shrewdness
Significance
Silence
Silliness
Simplicity
Sincerity
Skillfulness
Solidarity
Solitude
Sophistication
Soundness
Speed
Spirit
Spirituality
Spontaneity
Spunk
Stability
Status
Stealth
Stillness
Strength
Structure
Success
Support
Supremacy
Surprise

Sympathy
Synergy
Self-actualization
Strategic
Teaching
Temperance
Thankfulness
Thoroughness
Thoughtfulness
Timeliness
Traditionalism
Tranquility
Transcendence
Trust
Trustworthiness
Thrift
Tidiness
Truth
Teamwork
Tolerance
Truth-seeking
Understanding
Unflappability
Uniqueness
Unity
Usefulness
Utility
Valor
Variety
Victory
Vigor
Virtue
Vision
Vitality
Vivacity
Volunteering
Vision
Warm-heartedness
Warmth
Watchfulness
Wealth
Willfulness
Willingness
Winning
Wisdom

Wittiness
Wonder
Worthiness
Youthfulness
Zeal

Obviously, no one can live by 10-15 CORE values. The very word core means the central or most important parts. So, the next step in identifying your true purpose is isolating the top values that are most central to you living life on your terms as your authentic self.

Here's how—first, document all of the circled items from the above list. There are 15 spaces below for you to do this.

_____   _____   _____

_____   _____   _____

_____   _____   _____

_____   _____   _____

_____   _____   _____

Next, isolate the top 10 from the list above:

_____   _____

_____   _____

_____   _____

_____   _____

_____   _____

Then, from the top 10, what are the five from above that are most in line with how you see your life:

1. _____

2. _____

3. _____

4. _____

5. _____

Finally, place a number next to each of the above 5 to rank them in order of how you live your life. Place them in order below:

1. _____

2. _____

3. _____

4. _____

5. _____

Now that you've narrowed down your core value set, it's time to identify your true purpose. Leveraging the values that you ranked 1-5 above, you will create a purpose statement.

Take the values you ranked as your top 3 and construct a sentence that specifies your purpose. For example, my top 3 are fun, fulfilment and presence.

The purpose statement I created is as follows:

My purpose in life is to reveal the opportunity others have to live with a presence that creates more fun and fulfilment in their own lives.

Write your purpose statement below:

Characteristics

Your personal characteristics help create the experience and perspective in which you live. Exploring how you see yourself and learning more about how others perceive you can provide a better understanding of how aligned you are with your purpose. In addition, it may help expose additional growth opportunities.

1. **Purpose Alignment**—Now that you've identified or are closer to identifying your true purpose, we can examine the personal characteristics that help support it. If you are living life with purpose, the characteristics you display should fall in direct alignment with the purpose for which you live. The following activity helps establish how close you are to achieving purpose alignment.

If you had to describe yourself in three words, what would they be?

1. _____

2. _____

3. _____

What experiences in life helped create the characteristics you model?

```
┌─────────────────────────────────────────────────┐
│                                                   │
│                                                   │
│                                                   │
│                                                   │
│                                                   │
└─────────────────────────────────────────────────┘
```

Send an email to ten people asking them to describe you in three words.

Review the responses and identify what behaviors you have demonstrated that could have driven their perception.

```
┌─────────────────────────────────────────────────┐
│                                                   │
│                                                   │
│                                                   │
│                                                   │
│                                                   │
└─────────────────────────────────────────────────┘
```

Based on those responses, how would you say people experience you? Warm and fast, warm and slow, cold and fast, or cold and slow?

_____

What three words do you want people to describe you as?

1. _____

2. _____

3. _____

Revisiting the purpose you identified for yourself in a previous exercise, how do your characteristics described by you and those you emailed fall in alignment with the purpose you outlined?

Example: The purpose you identified was to be a beacon of light for those that live in the shadows. Folks describe you as introverted, witty, and kind.

The question for you to consider then is "Would you say these characteristics help drive your purpose of being a beacon of light?"

What three characteristics would help drive or support the purpose you specified?

1. _____

2. _____

3. _____

What behaviors should you incorporate in your life to ensure the manner you exhibit to others supports your purpose?

DOPE

As discussed in the DOPE 4 Bird Personality Test section of chapter 3, The Foundation of F.U.N., your personality plays a major role in how you experience relationships, life, and the creation of your perspective. Identifying the bird style with which you identify and understanding the elements of it can help answer many questions about your experiences in life.

1. **Your Bird Defined**—this activity will allow you to take a deeper look at your personality and how it drives your personal perspective.

Complete your personal bird assessment at www.richardstep.com.

What is your primary bird style?

If you identify with multiple bird styles, what is your secondary bird style?

Based on the content in chapter 3, The F.U.N. in Foundation, your bird assessment, and your own personal experience, if you had to list all the characteristics of your primary bird style, what would they be?

How might others receive or experience you based on the characteristics of the bird with which you've identified?

What difficulties might result from these personality traits?

What is one thing you can do TODAY to reduce the difficulties outlined above and potentially allow folks to experience you differently?

Understanding Others' Perspectives

Experiences Drive Others' Perspectives

As discussed in chapter 4, The F.U.N. in Understanding Others' Perspectives, a person's perspective largely comes from their experiences. That perspective is a key differentiator in us as human beings. Now that you have more insight into the elements that create your perspective, we can explore other people's perspectives and the elements that formed those perspectives.

1. **Why Are They Like That?**—Have you ever encountered someone whom you really appreciate? Someone so memorable that when you walk away from them, you wonder how they came to see things the way the do?

This activity is designed to help you dissect an individual's perspective and identify how you can use what you learn to close your own opportunity gaps.

Identify the most FUN individual in your life (work, friends, family, acquaintances, etc.):

_____

What characteristics do they display that led you to label them as FUN?

What do you know about their background or personal experience that helped shape the way they live life?

Seek this individual out in whatever communication modality you prefer, compliment them on displaying the characteristics that allowed you to recognize them as FUN, and ask them what experiences drove their outlook on life.

How could you incorporate some of the behaviors this person exhibits to help positively drive your perspective? (What is it they do that can be recreated by you in an authentic manner?)

2. **A Frustrating Experience**—When was the last time you encountered someone that you didn't necessarily appreciate. It could be someone you met in passing, someone you work with, a complete stranger, or even a family member. In this activity we will identify characteristics of others that may get under our skin and

how to reduce the negative impact of interactions with individuals who display them.

Identify an individual you feel brings stress in your life.

What are the characteristics this individual displays that may rub you the wrong way?

If you were to hold up a mirror, what is it that you could be doing in response to this individual that is driving what you see in them?

How could your response to this individual be causing frustration in you?

What can you do TODAY that will reduce the negative impact this person has on your day?

Examples could include but aren't limited to: asking yourself questions about what could be driving your experience (curious); jot down the interaction you desire with this individual and shift your mindset going in; or have an open conversation with this individual about their expectations of the relationship in hopes of connecting on a deeper level.

Name a time in the last month when you had a negative reaction to another individual.

List all the possibilities in that individual's life that could be driving the way you experience them.

How would you positively excuse the behavior? The bulk of people are inherently good, so how can you spin your experience with this individual to see the good in them?

What are some positive outcomes of this individual displaying the characteristics they do?

One example could include the following: you meet a physician who won't stop talking about how great they are and who expresses extreme confidence in their abilities. You are annoyed by their arrogance.

Upon reflecting you think to yourself that if indeed you ever needed a doctor for something serious, you would appreciate having one as confident in their abilities as the individual you just met.

3. **Curious vs. Furious**—There are two ways to approach any situation: curious or furious. You may recall that curious individuals look at someone's behavior and ask themselves what could be driving the outcome. Furious individuals, however, look at someone's behavior and make judgments as a result.

As you interact with individuals daily, are you more prone to ask yourself what's driving their behavior, or are you more likely to grow frustrated by their actions? Below are some examples of curious and furious approaches to situations.

Curious Approach	*Furious Approach*
What happened?	How could they?
How did we get here?	Why me?
What led to this?	What the hell?
Walk me through ...	I call shenanigans!

Below are three common scenarios in which you might find yourself. Under each, identify two curious and two furious approaches to the situation.

Situation 1—It is one of those nights where you don't feel like cooking, so you take the whole family out for dinner at a local restaurant. Once seated, it takes several minutes before your server greets you. The server appears to be distracted and isn't very friendly. The food takes longer than expected, and once it arrives, it is cold.

You eat at this restaurant regularly and have never had an experience quite like this one.

How do you respond?

Curious Approach #1:

Curious Approach #2:

Furious Approach #1:

Furious Approach #2:

Situation 2—You are working on a project at work that requires a deliverable or the help of another individual. Despite the fact that expectations were set, the person hasn't delivered on their task and the project is at risk of being delayed.

You haven't had much interaction with this individual since the original agreement was made and need to reach out.

How do your respond?

Curious Approach #1:

Curious Approach #2:

Furious Approach #1:

Furious Approach #2:

Situation 3—You get home from work, and the house is in disarray. There's a huge mess in the kitchen, you can hear arguing in another room, and no one is ready for the engagement everyone in the family knows will start at 7:00 p.m. It's 6:15 p.m. How do you respond?

Curious Approach #1:

Curious Approach #2:

Furious Approach #1:

Furious Approach #2:

Creating Meaningful Connections

Would you like to create more meaningful connections in life? Connections that could drive more fun and fulfillment in all that you do? As discussed previously, the bulk of our conversations with others are surface-level featuring topics like weather, family, or work. To truly drive meaningful connections and make more of an impact on those with whom you interact, it is imperative to show a genuine interest in them. The activities that follow feature questions that will help provoke thought and connection in conversation. When implemented, you'll find that your interactions drive stronger relationships in life.

1. **Noticing and Connecting Questions**—There are many different types of questions that can help drive conversation. Noticing and connecting questions are highly effective in showcasing a genuine interest in others. You may recall these questions being introduced earlier in chapter 4, The F.U.N. in Understanding Others' Perspectives. A refresher can be found below.

   Noticing questions are based off of things that you observe. For example, you might see an interesting item on a coworker's desk. Leveraging that observation you may ask, "I noticed a picture on your desk with a quote on it. What does it say?" Another example could pertain to something an individual is wearing. For example, "I noticed you wear bow-ties regularly, and I really like them. How many would you say you have?" Typically when you ask about things that interest others, they will be far more willing to engage with and appreciate you for taking the time to ask As a result, people feel valued, you feel better about the interaction, and you're both more likely to have a FUN experience.

   Other examples of noticing questions include:

   - I love your watch. Does it hold special meaning for you?

   - Tell me about your necklace. Was it a gift?

- I noticed the logo on your notebook. What is that from?

- I noticed you wear colorful socks. Is that an everyday thing?

Connecting questions are based off of like interests. These questions help form connections, build trust, and create a more FUN interaction. For example, you might spark a conversation by asking about a mutual friend, "I saw that you and I have several mutual connections on LinkedIn. How do you know Bob Smith?" Hobbies, sports, entertainment, restaurants, and education are all additional topics that could help provide a connection between two parties. Another example could sound something like, "Did I see you and your family over at that Italian restaurant off of 5th last week? We've been going there for years. What'd you think?"

Other examples of connecting questions include:

- My wife and I are in the market for a new SUV, and I see you drive a Tahoe. What do you like most about it?

- I see that you graduated from UCLA. I was class of 1998. Which year were you?

- What is your hometown? (If applicable) Do you know the Kussard family that's from there?

- It looks as though we're both Royals fans. What's your most notable Royals moment?

Now that you have a better understanding of noticing and connecting questions, complete the exercises below.

The next person you meet, pose a noticing question, such as, "I love your shoes. Where did you get them?" See if you can connect with them in some way by figuring out a person, thing, place, or want that you both have in common. Afterwards, notice the sense of fun you feel due to the connecting conversation you engaged in.

Walk around the office and identify as many things as possible that you have in common with others. You don't have to comment on them. Just identify the number of things of like interest that could be a topic of conversation. Once identified, reflect back on the number of discussions you've had with those coworkers in the past featuring the items you have in common. What did you learn that you hadn't considered before?

Pay close attention to your significant other and small details such as painted fingernails, a new sweater, haircuts, etc. Comment on them when you notice them.

Identify three individuals you don't know well or at all. Notice something they're wearing or doing that might spark a conversation, and make it happen. Get out of your comfort zone and leverage noticing questions to meet three new people!

2. **Deeper Conversations**—The following is a list of questions intended to create more depth in conversations. Leverage as many of them as you can to start a team meeting off in a fun way, learn more about a loved one, or just have more engaging interactions with others. Ask at least five today and check them off as you go!

   1. If you could remove fear from the equation, what's one thing you'd like to try?

2. If the average human life span were forty years, how would you live your life differently?

3. Tell me about the best vacation you've ever taken.

4. Who is somebody in your life that you really look up to?

5. We are seventy years young sipping piña coladas on the beach talking through the legacies that we left. How do you want yours to look?

6. What is something you're proud of that not many people know about you?

7. What do you do for FUN?

8. If someone close were to describe your personality in three words, what words would they choose? What words do you wish they'd choose?

9. Tell me about your favorite hobbies.

10. What is the funniest thing that's ever happened to you?

11. What was the first concert you attended?

12. Who was your favorite celebrity hero or crush growing up?

13. What are you working on to improve yourself right now?

14. If you were to write a book, what would it be about?

15. What is the most inspiring experience you have had in recent memory?

16. How do you like to be celebrated or appreciated?

17. What's one thing you've always wanted to do? What's holding you back?

18. If you could meet someone from history, who would it be?

19. What are the top five things you cherish most in your life?

20. What do you enjoy most about having kids?

21. What is something you have learned about yourself recently?

22. What is a project you have in mind that you'd love to get done this year?

23. What does success mean to you?

24. If someone were to ask you about the key to finding success, what would you say?

25. If life had no limits and you could have and do anything you want, what would you choose to have and what would you choose to do?

26. If a doctor gave you one year to live, what would you try to accomplish?

27. What do you absolutely love in life?

28. If you left your current life in order to pursue your dreams, what would you leave behind?

29. How do you want the next five years of your life to look?

Expectations and Motivators

In order to truly understand the perspectives of others, it is imperative that you take the time to learn more about their expectations and motivators. Expectations are oftentimes based on perspectives or past experiences. However, if you want to differentiate yourself and increase the probability of fulfilling others' expectations, clear communication is key. Remember that uncommunicated expectations cause preplanned resentments. Simply put, if you want better relationships in life, which will allow you a greater sense of contentment, take the time to learn the expectations of others while communicating your own.

Have you ever stepped back to ask yourself what motivates those closest to you? There are many different types of motivators for individuals. Money, recognition from others, love, material things, and self-respect are just a few of the motivators I've identified as being prominent in my circle of friends or family. Understanding the motivators of others will allow you to speak and act in terms that resonate with those around you. In doing so, individuals will feel appreciated and recognize you as someone that has their best interest at heart. Who doesn't want to surround themselves with individuals like that?

To learn more about the motivators of others, I recommend reading *The Five Love Languages* by Gary Chapman. It provides amazing insight and may help drive improvements in your personal relationships.

1. **Level-Setting Expectations** — Communicating your expectations and learning what others expect from you is never a bad thing. The following exercises are intended to create an environment where you have a better understanding of the expectations of others. The result

from this clarity around expectations is that everyone has a greater sense of fun and ease.

Ask your family members about what expectations they have for the weekend.

Ask your children what they expect to happen if they don't follow through on requests you make of them.

Ask a coworker about what expectations they have on a project.

Ask your coworkers or boss how they prefer giving and receiving feedback.

Ask your boss what expectations they have of you and share yours of them.

Talk to your spouse about their expectations of you in the relationship. What are your expectations of them?

Clarify the expectations of you and your spouse on an upcoming visit to or from your parents. Maybe it is an upcoming holiday or just a weekend trip. What does each of you expect?

2. **The Motivators of Others** — Having a strong understanding of the motivators of others can make or break a relationship. The following exercises will allow you better insight into how those around you are motivated.

   At a family dinner, have a conversation about what makes each individual happy. Each individual should name three things that bring happiness into their lives. Asking a follow-up question such as "Why?" or "How?" will provide additional understanding of each person's personal motivators.

Ask a family member what motivates them the most. If they were to achieve the ultimate success in life, how would it look or be defined?

Have your team or a handful of coworkers jot down eight of their biggest motivators on a piece of paper. Have them circle their top three. Of the three circled, ask them to identify the one that moves them the most.

DOPE

As we learned in previous chapters and exercises, Richard Step's DOPE 4 Bird Personality Test is a great way to learn more about yourself while providing a better understanding of others. You interact with doves, owls, peacocks, and eagles on a daily basis. Being able to identify the bird style of others and several other key elements of their personality will allow you the opportunity to build a stronger connection, which in turn will increase your overall feeling of fun—and theirs too!

1. **Work and Family Inventory** — Who do you surround yourself with and how are they unique? The following exercise allows you to take inventory of those with whom you interact daily. Having a better understanding of them and what makes them tick will provide you guidance on how to modify your communication style for maximum impact. You should complete this inventory for every member of your immediate family, your closest friends, and those with whom you work most closely. I've provided one example each for a family member, coworker, and friend.

EXAMPLE

Family member's name: *Victoria*

Relationship to you: *Daughter*

Three characteristics that describe them: *Witty, smart, driven*

Bird style: *Eagle*

Motivated by: *The idea of being successful in life. She could care less about what others think and wants to achieve her goals for her own personal fulfillment.*

How you can strengthen the relationship: Be more concise in my communication and only supply her with details that may be important to her. Give her more opportunities to express her thoughts or ideas on a situation before I express my own.

Family member's name:

Relationship to you:

Three characteristics that describe them:

Bird style:

Motivated by:

How you can strengthen the relationship:

Family member's name:

Relationship to you:

Three characteristics that describe them:

Bird style:

Motivated by:

How you can strengthen the relationship:

Family member's name:

Relationship to you:

Three characteristics that describe them:

Bird style:

Motivated by:

How you can strengthen the relationship:

Family member's name:

Relationship to you:

Three characteristics that describe them:

Bird style:

Motivated by:

How you can strengthen the relationship:

EXAMPLE

Coworker's name: *Jim*

Relationship to you: *My boss*

Three characteristics that describe them: *Disconnected, quirky, data-driven*

Bird style: *Owl*

Motivated by: *Results. Enjoys seeing numbers improve as a result of our direct actions.*

How you can strengthen the relationship: Proactively supply him with a weekly report including in it what I take from what the data shows. Talk less about all the things I can tell don't interest him.

Coworker's name:

Relationship to you:

Three characteristics that describe them:

Bird style:

Motivated by:

How you can strengthen the relationship:

Coworker's name:

Relationship to you:

Three characteristics that describe them:

Bird style:

Motivated by:

How you can strengthen the relationship:

Coworker's name:

Relationship to you:

Three characteristics that describe them:

Bird style:

Motivated by:

How you can strengthen the relationship:

Coworker's name:

Relationship to you:

Three characteristics that describe them:

Bird style:

Motivated by:

How you can strengthen the relationship:

EXAMPLE

Friend's name: *Shannon*

Relationship to you: *Neighborhood friend. We met just under a year ago.*

Three characteristics that describe them: *Fun, thoughtful, hilarious*

Bird style: *Peacock*

Motivated by: *Making others happy. Shannon appears to be lifted up by the spirits of others. When she makes someone else laugh or smile, she is on top of the world.*

How you can strengthen the relationship: Express my appreciation for her more regularly. Give her more opportunities to showcase her personality and humor by asking her questions about things I know interest her.

Friend's name:

Relationship to you:

Three characteristics that describe them:

Bird style:

Motivated by:

How you can strengthen the relationship:

Friend's name:

Relationship to you:

Three characteristics that describe them:

Bird style:

Motivated by:

How you can strengthen the relationship:

Friend's name:

Relationship to you:

Three characteristics that describe them:

Bird style:

Motivated by:

How you can strengthen the relationship:

Friend's name:

Relationship to you:

Three characteristics that describe them:

Bird style:

Motivated by:

How you can strengthen the relationship:

With whom do you relate most? With whom do you have the most friction or differences?

In the pages that follow you will learn how to escape the prison of your mind by focusing on things that make you laugh, smile, or give you strength. You won't have to wear a catsuit, and the techniques are really quite easy.

However, you must be deliberate in focusing on the things that lift you up and not those that tear you down. It will take commitment and most likely, support. If you're willing to make the investment, you're ready to move forward. You're now ready for fundamism in practice.

The FUNdamentals of Fundamism

There are millions of things you can do for FUN to generate strength and distance yourself from a negative mindset. Many people believe that our experiences in life help shape the person we become. Taking this into consideration, I know we cannot change a mindset overnight. It took decades to form our perceptions on life and our attitudes toward it.

By slowly introducing fundamism into your daily life, you will begin to see a shift in the way you view and experience your world. The philosophy of fundamism is based on incorporating very specific and tactical FUNdamentals to help drive additional fulfillment and FUN experiences so that your overall perspective on life becomes delight-filled and positive.

This program can be approached many different ways. One possible approach is take one FUNdamental per day and fully commit to incorporating it throughout the day. It may make sense to begin on a Monday to jumpstart your week on a positive note.

Engage yourself fully in the FUNdamental and embrace the experiences you encounter when implementing it. Once you have completed the first FUNdamental on day one, you can tackle the second on day two.

Focus your energy solely on the second FUNdamental until you feel its benefits outweighing the discomfort (or whatever you define as its cost of implementation). Remember that the goal in this approach is to take only one FUNdamental at a time until you are completely comfortable in its utilization.

Another approach could be to build upon each FUNdamental weekly. For example, you would begin your first FUNdamental on week one. By the end of the week, you should start to feel a little more comfortable and build some excitement around starting week two. In week two, instead of focusing solely on the second FUNdamental, you would incorporate what you learned in week one, as well as the second FUNdamental. This approach is a little more demanding than the first because you have more to focus on. My suggestion is to only go this route if you truly notice that the previous FUNdamental feels natural and is now a part of your daily routine.

You may find an approach outside of the two listed above that works better for you. Great! Whatever route you go, stretch yourself to a point of discomfort as when true growth takes place.

Find your pace, enjoy the journey, and try to experience things a little differently than you have in the past so that you find yourself smiling more, laughing more, and overall more satisfied.

There is a journal page following each FUNdamental. This is so you can jot down your thoughts, experiences, and emotions. This self-reflection at the end of the day (or throughout the week) will give you the ability to stay the course or alter your approach in the FUNdamentals that follow.

Please note that if you desire to change your attitude permanently, you have to be dedicated to the implementation of this program.

In order to understand what that dedication entails, let's establish the difference between being committed to something versus being compliant. If you are compliant in doing something, you are just doing it because you feel you have to and the moment you can cut a corner without someone looking or judging you, you will. If you are committed to do something, you are doing it because you feel that deep down in your heart it is the right thing to do and that you will see some benefit from giving it your all. When you dedicate yourself to fundamism, that's when your whole attitude, perspective, and experience of life permanently changes to the positive.

Before you continue to the next page, you must ask yourself, "Am I ready to make a change in my life? Am I ready to become the person I want to be, the person that makes a room brighten up when I walk into it or the person who can see what a gift life is and the difference I can make to others?"

If the answer to any of these questions is yes, then you are well on your way to living a life characterized by fun and contentment!

FUNdamental #1
Affirmations and Blessings

WHAT:

Start each day with an affirmation and end each day by counting your blessings.

WHY:

The beginning and end of each day are of pivotal importance in the grand scheme of your life. The beginning of the day will undoubtedly play some role in setting the tone for the coming day, and the end will influence your bedtime routine and sleeping patterns, which are directly related to your health, happiness, and wellbeing.

HOW:

It is so important to start your day with some positive reinforcement. And who better to provide that motivational kick-start than you?

The beauty of affirmations is that they are 100% customizable. They are designed by you to help you motivate and applaud yourself. Do you want a promotion at work? Do you aspire to have more confidence when dealing with the opposite sex? Are you proud of any qualities that you already possess?

Ask yourself what things need development in your life and which of your traits you want to acknowledge or compliment (yes, I said compliment—if you can't recognize and celebrate your individuality, why should anyone else?).

Put together a sentence or paragraph that praises and inspires you, look yourself in the mirror, and say it with gusto! If you believe in yourself (and you start each day by reminding yourself of that fact), there is no limit to what you can accomplish throughout the day and, in turn, your life.

An example of this might read, "I am in control of how I experience this day. I'm smart, funny, and have an uncanny ability to connect with others. I commit to bringing more FUN to this day, and there's nothing that will stand in my way!"

We have all been guilty at one point in our lives of taking things for granted. We have also had moments of epiphany where we realized that we loved or appreciated someone or something because of what they add to our lives.

In my case, those cathartic moments are generally followed by some guilt because I have not given the due recognition to those who have helped to improve the quality of my life.

In short, I have been remiss with regard to the words "thank you." Sometimes I am thanking an actual person, sometimes a higher power, and sometimes, I am thanking myself. No matter who is on the receiving end of my gratitude, it is important to identify my blessing and give thanks for it.

One example of this FUNdamental could be writing down a list of items for which you are grateful accompanied by what each means to you. By revisiting this list before going to sleep each night and adding or subtracting to it as you see fit, you'll find you are more present in identifying the good in your life and less focused on everything else.

This FUNdamental, in practice, is simple and quick. But by taking a few minutes at the end of each day to take stock and reflect on what made the day good, what you value about your life or others who are in it, what makes you happy and fulfilled, you are effectively stopping to smell the roses on the path of your life. Appreciation for what you have is an integral element of a happy existence.

FUNdamental #2
Pay Compliments

WHAT:

Pay a stranger or someone you do not speak with regularly a compliment.

WHY:

Dale Carnegie once said, "The kind words you and I say today we may forget, but the recipient just might remember them for a lifetime." When asking others if they receive enough recognition for the things they do, typically the response is an astounding, "NO!!!!!!" There is not a soul on the planet that does not enjoy receiving appreciation for the hard work and effort they put forth on a daily basis.

When you pay someone a compliment, you immediately see a change in their attitude. Smiles and a new confidence are usually the result of your kind words. It is not possible to know what everyone is going through in life or where they have been. However, by expressing your gratitude you might give someone the strength they were lacking to get through a difficult time.

While paying a compliment supplies the recipient with benefits, you also benefit! Your self-esteem will skyrocket with every smile you help to create. Relationships in your life will flourish as you begin to realize what an impact your ability to communicate has on those closest to you. You will start to feel a sense of accomplishment and joy that will help to carry you through even the most trying of times.

HOW:

We have hundreds of interactions with others every day. Accompanied with each interaction is the opportunity to express thanks. You might find that the young man working the drive-thru at your local coffee shop has a pleasant voice. Tell him.

You may be surprised by someone who waited several seconds to hold a door for you because they saw you walking up. Express a genuine thank you. Someone at work could be working on a cumbersome project and you notice the frustration on their face. Explain how beneficial their work is and show them appreciation for all of their efforts.

While the "what" in the compliment is important, don't forget the most critical aspect of giving compliments: the "why." You must explain the "why" in order to truly be effective. This can be done by expressing the importance of the recipient's actions or why they positively affect you.

Below is a brief example of an effective compliment. We will use a cashier from a local grocery store in this example.

She greets you with a big smile and asks you how your day is going. She seems sincere in her questions, and you can tell that she cares to know the answers. You notice her name badge says, "Stephanie." You might say something like this...

"It's not every day that you find someone who takes such great pride in helping others. I just want to say thank you, Stephanie, for caring, and keep up the great work!

This FUNdamental is easy to implement as you have so many opportunities throughout the day. Start with one compliment a day and build upon your momentum. When your confidence starts to grow, increase the number of compliments to two a day.

The more smiles you help to create, the better you will feel about yourself and your ability to influence others.

Remember there is always a learning curve associated when tackling something new. You could be uncomfortable at first. It's OK! Continue to stretch yourself and expand your comfort zone.

With time and practice this FUNdamental will get easier.

FUNdamental #3
Listen to Music with a Purpose

WHAT:

Listen to music with a purpose.

WHY:

Music is a lot of things to lots of different people. I'm not a musician, but I wish I was. To me, music makes me FEEL. Anything I want to feel, I can find a song that will help evoke that emotion. Like many of you reading this, I can think of numerous defining moments in my life and associate each memory with a song. Below is the most impactful example I recall.

The year was 2013. I was living in Portland, Oregon, with my wife, Melissa, and our eight-month-old daughter, Adalyn Grace. The moment I woke, I checked my phone to find in excess of ten phone calls and thirty texts. My father, just two weeks removed from his sixtieth birthday, had unexpectedly passed in his sleep.

A weird feeling came over me.

I was numb and knew I had to make plans to get home to Kansas City to help my family in the grieving process while making arrangements for his funeral services.

After exploring flights to KC, we came to the conclusion that driving would be more fiscally responsible than purchasing plane tickets.

We began our drive in the evening in hopes of allowing our baby girl some sleep to lessen her level of discomfort during such a trek. It had been a day since my father's passing, and I still hadn't shed a tear.

It was pitch black as I drove through Utah with my headphones on as my wife and daughter slept in the back. My iPod, stocked full of 10K songs from just about every genre, was on shuffle when it happened.

Death Cab for Cutie's "I Will Follow You into the Dark" came on, and I completely lost it. As tears rolled down my face, I was taken by the words of the song and was forced to come to grips with the loss of my father. It was therapeutic, and I needed that release. Music gave me the power to FEEL.

In a 2010 Los Angeles Times article (which you can read here: http://articles.latimes.com/2010/mar/01/health/la-he-0301-brain-music-therapy-20100301), Harvard neurologist Dr. Gottfried Schlaug explained that when an area of the brain is disabled due to trauma or disease, music provides a unique way to reach that area, sometimes restoring impaired functions such as movement, memory, and speech.

There is also evidence that suggests that music can offer help to patients who suffer from pain, depression, heart problems, immune system issues and a rapidly growing list of ailments.

Is it not then a foregone conclusion that music has healing properties?

Perhaps we could even consider it a kind of medicine (a completely harmless and easily accessible medicine that we have unlimited access to 24 hours a day, without a prescription). Eureka!

So, why in the world would we not avail ourselves of this miracle drug?

While we are not exercising this FUNdamental to deal with serious illness, we are most certainly exercising it to engage our brains and provide a therapeutic and uplifting experience that can help us to relax, smile, or get motivated.

HOW:

This FUNdamental is super easy to incorporate into your day. When I wake up in the morning, I turn on the shower, followed by my favorite Spotify playlist. Depending on the emotion I want to feel, I have the selection that will set the tone for my day.

Every day, without fail, it wakes me up and puts a spring in my step as I prepare for the events to follow. My family also enjoys Hall & Oats dance parties, and we frequently have YouTube music videos playing at our house throughout the day.

Our children LOVE music, and we can definitively see a change in them when it's playing.

Whether you are showering, driving to work, exercising, or even relaxing at home, you can add a little music to the mix. It can act as an energizer or a relaxant. You choose the mood you are aiming for, pick some appropriately paced music, and it will do the rest.

Remember that the FUNdamental is "Listen to Music with a Purpose."

I challenge you to choose your music wisely based on what you want to *feel* rather than just turning on the radio and allowing the DJ to direct your day.

FUNdamental #4
Exercise!

WHAT:

Exercise.

WHY:

The bulk of society understands the physical benefits of exercising on a regular basis.

According to www.nutristrategy.com, thirty minutes of physical activity, five days a week can reduce blood pressure, prevent heart disease, lower the risk of stroke, reduce the risk of osteoporosis, prevent back pain, reduce the risk of developing diabetes, prevent obesity, and countless other health benefits.

What many people don't know is that exercising regularly can also play a significant role in developing mental stability and promoting overall happiness.

A team of researchers at Duke University recently conducted a study monitoring those who suffered from depression. The researchers monitored participants for a period of four months and found that 60% of those who exercised for thirty minutes a day, three times a week conquered their depression without the use of prescription medication.

The amazing thing about this study is the success rate in overcoming depression was the exact same for those who only took prescription medication! Millions of people spend countless dollars on prescription antidepressants annually.

According to this study, the same outcome of reducing depression could be had for free just by going on walks a couple of times a week!

British statesman, Edward Stanley once said, "Those that think they have not time for bodily exercise will sooner or later have to find time for illness."

Exercising throughout the week can promote not only physical health but will ultimately lead to regular smiles and a positive mindset.

HOW:

You don't have to be a gym rat or have a monthly membership to an expensive health club to exercise regularly. Anyone can spend five minutes exploring exercise techniques on the internet search engine of their choice to find a routine that can be performed in the comfort of their own home.

Regardless of whether we have a personal trainer, watch hours of late-night infomercials featuring P90X or Insanity, have our own Bowflex in the basement, or just go for a jog around the block, we all have the capability of getting our sweat on!

Exercise doesn't have to be as difficult and involved as we sometimes make it. Grab your iPod or MP3 player, step out your front door, and take in the sites of your neighborhood as you enjoy some good music and a peaceful walk.

FUNdamental #5
Let It Go!

WHAT:

Release yourself of negative thoughts, anxiety, or depression created by previous experience or heartache.

WHY:

It is an unfortunate, but true fact that we humans are plagued by negativity throughout our daily lives. Whether office politics, community problems, a fellow driver with a bad case of road rage, or a more personal issue has got you down, negativity is an unavoidable fact of life.

Fortunately for us, we have a choice.

We can choose not to get mired in it and refocus our energy on happier things. We can choose to be forgiving instead of petty, cheerful instead of whiny, and we can move on instead of dwelling on adversity.

This is a multi-faceted FUNdamental because in practice, it incorporates both internal and external adjustments to your attitude. It requires you to stop indulging the part of your brain that wants to relive or obsess about bad things and to talk yourself into letting it all go.

This FUNdamental, in short, is about being the bigger person with other people and when necessary, yourself!

Releasing negativity can change the tone of your day, and, in effect, your life. You will be able to enjoy work, social outings, and basic errands a whole lot more if you can learn to ignore people's bad attitudes and silence the discouraging noise the world is throwing at you.

Self-talk is an important component of exercising this FUNdamental properly. Patterns of negative self-talk are generally something that can begin as early as childhood. Not only do they serve as a vehicle for depression and self-defeat, but they can actually decrease our productivity.

So it stands to reason that if we change the pattern of chatter going on inside us, we can see real results in how we experience life on the outside.

HOW:

First, it is important to recognize how often you are contemplating or even anticipating bad things to happen over the course of a day. Once you have identified the frequency with which you incorporate these debilitating thoughts, you can begin the process of mitigating their control over you.

I am of the opinion that if you say something enough, you can talk yourself into believing it. Therefore, the more you tell yourself bad things are going to happen, the more you experience bad things happening!

Oftentimes, great things are happening all around you, but you don't even notice if you've trained your brain to expect only negativity.

So how do you change?

We first need to replace those negative thoughts with positive ones. Take notice of how you are phrasing things and make note of them in a journal.

Are you using a lot of phrases like "I can't," "I won't," or "I don't"? Turn those negative statements into motivating questions. For instance, "I can't do this" can be changed to "How can I do this?" If negative self-talk is creating outcomes that generate misery, rephrasing statements to drive a more positive mindset is key to delivering a different life experience.

Another important aspect of this FUNdamental is letting go of things that persistently plague you.

While past experiences can prove powerful learning tools in avoiding previous mistakes, it is hard to move forward if you're consistently looking in the rearview mirror. Life is full of challenges. Some are far worse than others.

Whether you've experienced the terrible loss of a loved one, a traumatic event, made a terrible decision, fell out with a friend, or anything else that is consistently weighing heavily on your mind, you have to let it go.

Take time to grieve, think about what you learned from the experience, even provide yourself time to appreciate the greatness that was offered as a result of that individual or situation—and then LET IT GO!

Think about one individual you haven't communicated with in a while. They were once a close friend, family member, or someone with whom you enjoyed interacting. For some reason, you stopped. You had a disagreement, they said something you didn't like, or something came between you. Let it go.

Pick up your phone right now and drop them a line. Text, call, or email this individual, and tell them you're thinking of them and the fun they once brought to your life. Do so without expectation of how, if, or when they respond, and feel the release of an old hurt.

In closing, there is no way to avoid negativity altogether. However, if you practice the Let It Go FUNdamental, confining these negative experiences to short-term memory and incorporating some positive self-talk, you'll be in awe how differently you'll experience life.

So LET IT GO ALREADY!

FUNdamental #6
Make Yourself Laugh

WHAT:

Find ways to make yourself laugh.

WHY:

"Humor is the great thing, the saving thing. The minute it crops up, all of our irritations and resentments slip away and a sunny spirit takes their place." —Mark Twain

While many of us have heard that laughter is the best medicine for what ails us, I believe Mark Twain truly captured the definition of humor and how it positively affects us in his quote above.

According to Paul E. McGhee, PhD, "Your sense of humor is one of the most powerful tools you have to make certain your daily mood and emotional state support good health."

Those that laugh regularly know that it helps spark energy, regulates pain, reduces stress, and even strengthens the immune system!

Laughter is contagious. When one person laughs, others tend to follow suit. No one wants to be the person that gets others down. Humor is one sure fire way to positively impact not only yourself but others, as well.

HOW:

There are countless ways to make yourself or others laugh. Sharing embarrassing moments, telling jokes, doing silly dances with friends, or watching comedy television are just a few ways to get that funny bone tickled.

Every Friday night on Comedy Central, stand-up comics perform on a show called "Comedy Central Presents." By setting my DVR recorder to record this entire series, I can generate a laugh whenever I need to just by pressing "play."

Another avenue to explore when trying to get a chuckle is to laugh at yourself. There is no better time to act ridiculous than when no one else is around. When we are alone, no one is around to judge us but ourselves.

For years, I worked as a call center representative who had to fix people's "problems" on a daily basis. It seemed as though everyone who called me was mad at the world and needed me to turn their situation around.

Hearing negative experiences day in and day out can really take a toll on an individual's mindset. Following a long and tiresome day, I would always try to find ways to cleanse myself of the negativity that surrounded me at work.

One of my favorite ways of accomplishing this was to drop my things at the door upon my arrival home and sprint to my bedroom. Once my bed was in sight, I would leap onto it with my arms and legs fully extended.

Those of you familiar with wrestling may remember a wrestler by the name of Eddie Guerrero. It was his move known only as "the frog splash" that turned my day around.

You see, when I dropped my "baggage" at the door and made the leap into my bed, I felt silly. I even remember saying out loud, "Paul, you're an idiot!" However, no one was around to judge me, and ultimately, I felt completely different about myself and my day. It was as though I had taken a bath in positivity!

Other ways that have helped me to laugh at myself are dancing before the mirror, making up songs, and talking to myself. I don't believe that there is any one way that is better than another for the implementation of this FUNdamental.

If it makes you laugh, then do it often!

FUNdamental #7
Meditate/Relax

WHAT:

Take time out of your busy day to relax or meditate.

WHY:

Have you ever lain down for bed at the end of a busy day and were unable to sleep as your brain was overwhelmed with thoughts of things to do or worries out of your control?

Join the club!

One can argue that the reason this happens is due to the fact that we are always preoccupied with the things going on throughout our day. When we don't take time to ourselves to clear our minds and focus solely on our own personal wellbeing, our brain takes over when our day slows down. This, of course, usually being the time we lay ourselves down to sleep.

Per an article written by Psychology Today called, "The Benefits of Meditation," those that meditate "shift negative brain waves in the stress prone right frontal cortex of the brain to the calmer left frontal cortex."

Unfortunately, I am no doctor so I struggle understanding what this statement means. Luckily the article breaks it down to explain that when you meditate, a mental shift happens in the brain such that there's a significant reduction in the likelihood of stress, anxiety, and depression.

HOW:

There are numerous resources in the world today dedicated to meditation including the how to, benefits of, and whys surrounding its value. A couple of our favorites are Stephan Bodian's *Meditation for Dummies* and Victor Davich's *8 Minute Meditation.*

Meditation for Dummies includes an audio CD with short meditation exercises that you can download to an iPod or MP3 player. You can do these exercises when you awake from your slumber, in the sauna at the gym, during lunch in the office, or right before bed.

8 Minute Meditation focuses on meditation for the beginner and those constantly on the run. The book quickly gives you exercises and explains why they are important. It allows you to experience the power of meditation simply by doing.

The only way to believe in something is to experience it ourselves. *8 Minute Mediation* allows you the chance to determine whether meditation is right for you in minutes.

As I am not a meditation expert, I don't want to give too much info on how to meditate. However, a good friend of mine painted a picture of how he incorporates meditation in his daily life.

Below you will find his instruction:

- Find a quiet place where you will not be interrupted, and get comfortable.

- Close your eyes and focus on your breathing. Feel the oxygen fill your lungs.

- As you exhale, imagine letting go of all the anxiety and worry in your life.

- While continuing to focus on your breath, picture yourself floating to the bottom of a body of water. As your weighted body sinks further down, look up to where you originally entered the water.

- Picture your worry and the troubles in your life getting further and further away from you as you left them when you took the plunge.

- Breathe easily and continue to focus on the oxygen entering and filling your body. As you plummet further into the water, embrace the clarity of your mind as your thoughts were left far above you.

Remember what Travis Kelce stated in the foreword of this book?

"As you reflect, find comfort in revisiting the past. Yes, you'll feel some pain but reliving how you felt through your worst moments can help keep you on track. It keeps your mind in a place where you're motivated to make sure you never get back to that point again.

The key to growth is pushing through the heartache without wallowing in it and developing a plan to move yourself forward."

While meditating, embrace your thoughts as they help identify your foundation, then work to clear your mind of all things so as to find the right path to your own enlightenment.

FUNdamental #8
Read

WHAT:

Read something of interest.

WHY:

When I was a kid, my mother always told me that reading made me smart. For years I thought intelligence was directly correlated to the number of books I read.

Maybe that's why Forrest Gump's "I'm not a smart man" quote always resonated with me.

Dr. Seuss once wrote, "The more that you read, the more things you will know. The more that you learn, the more places you'll go." I knew that reading would provide me opportunity, but it was not something that I enjoyed or gave me strength. As a result, I found myself gravitating towards other FUNdamentals like working out, video games, playing basketball, and more.

As I grew older, I realized that there are far more benefits to reading than just growing my vocabulary or feeling smart, mental health being the most important to me.

A 2013 article from *The Atlantic* titled, "More Scientific Evidence That Reading Is Good for You," details how reading reduced the rate of cognitive decline in dementia patients. In addition, the article outlines how reading can provide individuals with "an increased tolerance for uncertainty."

One of the most powerful articles on the benefits of reading for me was a *Huffington Post* column titled, "6 Science-Backed Reasons to Go Read a Book Right Now," written by Laura Schocker.

Laura stated that reading can reduce stress, keep the brain sharp, reduce the risk of Alzheimer's disease, help you sleep better, make you more empathetic, and ease depression.

What more evidence do we need?

I know reading is not always as F.U.N. as binge watching Netflix. However, if reading can improve mental health as outlined above, why not give it a try?

HOW:

There are millions of pieces of literature that can be found anywhere including the checkout counter at a local grocery store, the library, or at the click of a button from the comfort of your own home. My mother, Martha, goes to the library every Saturday morning, checks out three novels, reads them all in a week's time, and returns them the following Saturday to repeat the cycle.

I'm not that diligent or driven to read at that level. Typically, I enjoy reading sports, feel-good stories, or news articles from links I find on Twitter.

For me, it's important to avoid strongly opinionated articles or those written with a negative tone. As a motivational speaker, I always thought I had to read self-help content to stay relevant in my industry. However, when I read that type of content, typically I lose interest within minutes.

As you begin or continue your exploration into the FUNdamental of reading, it's imperative that you balance the things you think you should read with those that are actually of interest. This will improve the likelihood of you enjoying reading while reducing the probability of burnout.

Tonight as you finally find time to wind down and are looking for a little mental relief, try substituting the remote for a good read. If the result is a great night's rest and a temporary escape from your troubles, you'll be thankful you did.

FUNdamental #9
Stretch

WHAT:

Get your stretch on or try some yoga.

WHY:

Now I'm not the most flexible gentleman on the planet. However, when I get a good stretch in, I typically end up feeling more relaxed, mentally fit, and at peace with my surroundings. After three knee surgeries, I've found that stretching can ease the pain created by changes in weather pressure or physical activity.

Being more bendy is an added bonus, if you get my drift.

K. Aleisha Fetters, in her Fitness Magazine column titled, "11 Seriously Awesome Benefits of Stretching," wrote that, "stretching primes your muscles for exercise, improves your posture, eases back pain, improves exercise form, prevents injury, boosts joint health, slashes stress, helps you sleep better, boosts blood flow to your brain, improves energy, and fights nagging anxieties."

Oftentimes we consider stretching as a precursor to an activity or something to be incorporated after exercise. As you can see from the benefits above, stretching doesn't have to apply exclusively to pre-or post-workouts. Stretching itself can be the activity.

Challenge yourself to a good stretch and feel the difference in your physical and mental health!

HOW:

Try touching your toes (just give your legs a hug if you can't), bring your knees to your chest while lying on the floor, make a butterfly with your legs to stretch the groin, grab your elbow over your head to stretch your triceps, and grab a door jam stretching your arm behind you to work those pectorals.

There are a million resources out there for guidance on stretching.

Take a yoga class, check out a book from the library, or do an old-fashioned internet search on "easy stretches."

Grab a family member, coworker, or friend to give you a hand, and don't push yourself too hard. You'll want to feel some sensation but not excruciating pain. Thirty to forty-five seconds per stretch and just two or three stretches total is typically a good way to get the blood flowing.

If you're not used to stretching, be patient with yourself. As stated before, I'm not the most flexible.

However, setting aside a few minutes a day to get my stretch on has produced countless benefits, and I'm getting more limber by the day. Have F.U.N. and happy stretching!

FUNdamental #10
Smile!

WHAT:

Make yourself smile.

WHY:

Bobby McFerrin once sang, "Don't worry, be happy. Cause when you worry, your face will frown and that will bring everybody down, so don't worry, be happy (now)."

It was a popular and uplifting song for a very specific reason.

Though a smile isn't generally going to be a cure-all for what's nagging at you, the domino effect of the impression it leaves on others can actually make you feel better.

A smile will always emit a positive vibe and lighten the mood, so it stands to reason that most people will respond in kind when they see a smile. So, not only does a smile have the power to improve your disposition, it can bring delight to others too.

What a simple and powerful tool, right?

It should also be noted that smiles should not be reserved for people we know. Strangers on the street and service people will appreciate a smile just as much as your mom or best friend.

Have you ever flashed a smile at the cashier at the grocery store or the person working a drive-thru window? If not, try it! If you want to be really daring, take a look at this individual's nametag and address them by name. The results will be just as rewarding (if not more) as flashing your pearly whites at a good buddy.

You'll be surprised at the reaction you get, as many employees don't get treated kindly. The pleasure that they get from being appreciated for the help they are offering is immeasurable.

Understandably, the notion that a simple smile can actually make you feel better sounds a little silly, but believe it or not, science has actually proven it! So have a little faith in those cognitive studies and remember that when you are feeling blue, your attitude and mindset can be shifted by simply "turning that frown upside down."

HOW:

What makes you smile? Do more of that and less of what doesn't. It's really that simple.

Go for a walk, make someone laugh, eat your favorite food, accomplish a goal, listen to your favorite song, watch a funny YouTube video, go play catch with your child, or do anything else that brings you happiness.

Any one of the aforementioned items can be a FUNdamental by themselves. However, the goal here is to immediately do whatever has the highest probability of making YOU smile. Get to it!

Additional FUNdamentals

The purpose of *fundamism* is to get you to gravitate towards the things that give YOU strength. In order to change your life perspective to one characterized by delight and fulfillment, you have to explore which FUNdamentals work best for you.

Not everyone would be comfortable throwing on a cat wrestling singlet and going to a Major League Baseball game. Some of you might not even enjoy the detailed FUNdamentals outlined above.

The goal here is for you to try things that might bring a little more fun and happiness into YOUR life. Get comfortable being uncomfortable and live a little!

Below are 100 additional FUNdamentals that can be incorporated into your home or work life. If you haven't found one or ten that resonate with you yet, your journey is just beginning. There are millions of FUNdamentals out there, and I'd love to write about them all. This is just the start.

If you have things that you do for FUN and provide strength, the fundamism community would appreciate hearing from you.

Visit www.fundamism.com, our Facebook page, Twitter account, or any other communication outlet you can find to post your FUNdamentals.

Remember the words of Keith Harrell, "Growing up, someone in life gave you so many smiles. If someone doesn't have one, bless them with one of your own."

Sharing your FUNdamental might be the very thing that gets someone else through a challenging time.

Have FUN!

Number 1: Think of times when you were most happy in life. Write down your top ten memories.

Number 2: Find a local playground and swing on the swings. How high can you go?

Number 3: Share one thing you genuinely admire about as many people as you can without telling them what you're doing.

Number 4: Set a goal of smiling for a specific amount of time. Start off with five to ten minutes and see if you can top it later in the day.

Number 5: Learn the names of others. When placing a call to a business or being waited on anywhere, ask the individual you're speaking with for their name. Then use their name throughout the conversation.

Number 6: Start each day with an affirmation. Jot down something you admire about yourself and how you envision the day being a success.

Number 7: End each day by counting your blessings. Ask a friend or family member the best thing to happen to them that day followed by sharing your own.

Number 8: Call or visit a loved one. Tell them what you appreciate about them and that you love them.

Number 9: Watch something funny like a stand-up comedy special, movie, or show.

Number 10: Search the internet for new jokes or funny stories.

Number 11: Listen to your favorite podcast or one that interests you.

Number 12: Be helpful to someone in need. Carry someone's groceries, lend a hand on a project, or just be there when they need you most. Be selfless. Look to help them solely because it makes them feel good and because you know it's the right thing to do. DO NOT EXPECT TO BE GIVEN SOMETHING IN RETURN.

Number 13: Volunteer or donate to a cause that moves you.

Number 14: Create a to-do list, check off tasks as they're completed, and reward yourself when accomplishments are met. Create a point system for yourself or take time out to reflect on your accomplishments once you complete items.

Number 15: Go someplace you have never been or try something new.

Number 16: Voice your appreciation when people do things for you. Express genuine sincerity when saying thanks and tell them WHY it was important to you.

Number 17: Progressive learning. Challenge yourself to learn something new every day. Research crazy facts, the history of people that interest you, cook a new dish, explore a new hobby, etc.

Number 18: Hang out with a friend(s).

Number 19: Turn off your phone and email for one hour. Take time for yourself without distractions and be present.

Number 20: Be cordial. For one day, say hello or good day to everyone that makes eye contact. Spark up conversation with a stranger.

Number 21: Enjoy your favorite meal.

Number 22: Play a game. It can be a video game, card game, or a sport with friends or family. Want to have even more fun? Make up your own new game!

Number 23: Express confidence. Force yourself to be more assertive and sure of yourself. Wear bright colored socks, approach people you do not typically interact with, tell your family something you are proud of that you accomplished in the day, and more.

Number 24: Be environmentally conscious. Pick up trash on the street, volunteer to clean up a park or garden, etc.

Number 25: Write down your thoughts. Keep a diary or journal, and reflect regularly.

Number 26: Let go of a fear. Release yourself of an inhibition or conquer a fear. Ride a roller coaster, dance in public, sing in front of others, or do something you have thought about for years but never had the courage to do.

Number 27: Get organized. Organize your closet, your contact list, email, etc.

Number 28: Envision your future and develop a plan to make it happen. Dream big. What are the three things you can do within the next week to get closer to accomplishing your goal?

Number 29: Give yourself a gift. Take a vacation day to yourself, buy a splurge item, treat yourself to your favorite dish, etc.

Number 30: Pay it forward. Pay someone's toll, buy coffee for the next person in line, pick up the tab at dinner, etc.

Number 31: Appreciate or acknowledge the little things. Smell the flowers, listen to your friends or family laughing, observe how beautiful/handsome your spouse is, and more.

Number 32: Find someone to talk with. Talk about everything or anything with someone in your life. Express your thoughts or opinions to a good listener.

Number 33: Release negativity that's been plaguing you. Forgive a friend or make peace with an old issue that's been bothering you. Call them or schedule a meeting.

Number 34: Steer clear of gossip or negative talk.

Number 35: Self-talk. Talk to yourself throughout the day. Give yourself positive feedback, ask yourself questions, or pump yourself up.

Number 36: Ask to speak with someone's superior and let the superior know the person did their job really well.

Number 37: Speak with a smile. Mama always told you, it is not what you say but how you say it. Communicate with a smile and see how much of a difference it makes.

Number 38: Paint a picture. It can be something basic like a rainbow or something complex like the Mona Lisa. Whatever you choose, just enjoy being creative and artistic.

Number 39: Take a yoga class or try a few poses from the internet.

Number 40: Improv. Use your imagination at a team meeting or family gathering, and get everyone involved. You can do an internet search of "improv games" and find tons of examples or create your own.

Number 41: Show a genuine interest in others by asking open-ended questions to learn more about them. Try asking coworkers or family members things that you may not know about them.

Number 42: Hide-and-seek. Get a crew of family, friends, or coworkers together and let the fun begin.

Number 43: Photography. Identify a few places, people, or moments you would like to capture. Try using different filters, captions, angles, and more to add flavor to the imagery.

Number 44: Wear a costume while performing a daily task. Wear an old Halloween outfit to the grocery store and act like it's just a normal day.

Number 45: What's the best thing that's happened to you today? Write it down and revisit it on a day when things aren't going your way. As your day evolves and better things happen, write them down too!

Number 46: Create a game at work. Call center bingo, Jeopardy-style learning, coworker trivia, alphabet games where one coworker identifies a fun word starting with the letter A then moves down the line with the next coworker and letter. Research "fun games at work" or come up with your own.

Number 47: Water balloon fight. Fill up fifty to a hundred water balloons and invite neighbors or coworkers to join in. Line up in rows in front of partners and see how far you can play catch with a water balloon without it breaking (this is also super fun with a raw egg).

Number 48: Go for a walk and identify the things you appreciate along the path.

Number 49: Write a thank-you note to internal/external customers, employees, family, or anyone you think is deserving.

Number 50: Make a craft for someone you care about. Do an internet search for ideas or come up with your own.

Number 51: Send a funny meme to your friends.

Number 52: High five the next five people you see and tell them to have a great day.

Number 53: While doing an activity or working as a collective group, allow each person in the group to choose a song to listen to. Ask each group member why they selected that song and what it means to them.

Number 54: Take a nap. Find a cozy spot and get some rest.

Number 55: Get a massage. Ask a family member or pay an expert. I get full body reflexology every month, and it costs around $45/hour.

Number 56: Color a picture. Find an adult coloring book or create your own. When was the last time you played with crayons?

Number 57: Board game night. Invite family or neighbors over and have a ball. Whoever hosts gets to choose the game. This can also be done in the office over a team meeting.

Number 58: Spontaneous road trip. Pack a small bag, grab the family, and get out of dodge! Identify places you would like to visit within a 400-mile radius and make it happen.

Number 59: Take a bath. Candles, some good music, and your favorite beverage. Men, do not be too proud. I take baths on the reg, and they are WONDERFUL.

Number 60: Share funny stories. What is the funniest thing that has ever happened to you? Task a few individuals in your circle to write down their most memorable two to three, and share them over lunch.

Number 61: Visit a museum and create your own stories of how the artist got the inspiration for each piece.

Number 62: Sing a song. It can be one of your favorites or something you make up. No one is listening to you, so belt it out!

Number 63: Write a poem. Never done it before? Who cares! Find words that rhyme and throw them together in a few phrases. See what happens.

Number 64: Find a quote that speaks to you and live by it for a day.

Number 65: Put together a bowl of random phrases, pull one daily, and use it seamlessly in conversation.

Number 66: Create a competition. Whatever you come up with, energy is created when competing against yourself or others.

Number 67: Text five people in your contact list and tell them what you appreciate about them.

Number 68: Cloud pictures. Observe clouds in the sky with a friend, coworker, or family member. Use your imagination and tell each other what pictures you see.

Number 69: Be present and observe ten things around you at this moment that you appreciate

Number 70: Jump! When something good happens — someone tells you something exciting — you leave work for the day, or anything else that merits it, jump. Feel the spirit of a being a child again and literally jump for joy.

Number 71: Go camping in your backyard. Grab a tent, some blankets, ingredients for s'mores, and a creative mind for storytelling.

Number 72: Build an indoor fort. This is still one of my all-time favorites. Grab pillows, blankets, and anything else you can find around the house to make the most boss fort possible.

Number 73: Buy half a dozen shakes or frappes, and recruit five other people to have a speed-drinking competition. Make sure someone photographs the brain freeze moments.

Number 74: Secretly place sticky note happy faces on your coworkers' office space. Never tell who is responsible.

Number 75: Nerf battle. Blonds vs. brunettes, solid colors vs. non-solid colors, men vs. women, leadership team vs. direct reports. You choose the teams, just make it fun.

Number 76: For your next department meeting, have everyone take a selfie and leverage it to draw a self-portrait. Hang them in a common space and have other departments guess who each portrait is.

Number 77: Bring a blender and ingredients to work to make smoothies. Make one afternoon a smoothie afternoon and deliver small cups of smoothies to your coworkers, complete with Reddi-wip.

Number 78: Word of the day. Think *Pee-wee's Playhouse.* Decide amongst a group on a crazy word like "discombobulated," and see how many times you can work that word into conversation for the day. Highest total number of uses wins.

Number 79: Create a cardboard cutout of yourself that is life-size, and place it in your desk chair whenever you leave your office.

Number 80: Challenge some coworkers to a dollar store lunch. Everyone goes to the dollar store, can spend no more than five dollars, and reveals their lunch when they get back to the office. It will probably be mildly disgusting and fun!

Number 81: Start your next meeting by having everyone share their favorite movie line done in the best voice impression possible.

Number 82: Surprise everyone at work or at home with ice cream and all the fixings for an ice cream sundae party. This makes for a great pick-me-up in the afternoon and gets everyone talking and connecting.

Number 83: Blow up a watermelon in the parking lot at work.

Number 84: Organize remote control car races in the hallways of your office.

Number 85: While sitting at your desk answering emails, wear a giant foam cowboy hat. See how many people comment on it.

Number 86: Partner up with a coworker and dress as each other for a day.

Number 87: Teach yourself a new dance. Macarena, dougie, electric slide, whip and nae nae, or a good-old-fashioned running man. Why dance like no one's watching when you can show off your skills? So many individuals have a fear of dancing or say they have no rhythm. Dancing doesn't have to be about showing how skilled you are, just have fun. The Footloose kids from Bomont had a blast—you can too!

Number 88: Go stargazing. Take the family outside where stars can be seen at their brightest.

Number 89: Attend an afternoon movie by yourself. You can go with someone you care about, if you'd like. Just take in an afternoon show and avoid the crowded theatre. It's amazing how peaceful movies are during weekdays.

Number 90: Leverage your creativity to make up a story to tell your children or spouse.

Number 91: Play in a sprinkler. Don't overthink it. If you see a sprinkler, stop what you're doing and run through it!

Number 92: Have a picnic. Make your own or grab some takeout on the way. Find a relaxing spot and have a relaxing lunch outside.

Number 93: Family dance party! Have each family member pick a song and everyone has to dance. Who cares what you look like? The goal is to have fun together!

Number 94: Buy or pick some flowers for a loved one. When delivered, tell them the flowers are just because you appreciate them.

Number 95: Play catch with a friend or family member using a football, baseball, or anything you see fit.

Number 96: Go to the zoo and make up human names for each animal.

Number 97: Identify an individual that could use a lighthearted conversation and make it happen.

Number 98: Have individuals submit photos of each other and have a caption contest. Funniest caption wins!

Number 99: Find a recipe that sounds good and make it. Beginner, intermediate, or advanced chefs can all enjoy cooking a good meal (or at least eating one!).

Number 100: Create your own version of *Family Feud*. "We asked Steve from accounting the top five answers for the best movies of all time and his answers are . . . ?" This is a good way to see how well you know your coworkers or family while having a fun time.

FUN Chapter Takeaways

- Exploring your own personal foundation and completing the foundation exercises will provide a better understanding of the control YOU have in driving more FUN in life. Stop making excuses and look inward to determine what's necessary for self-improvement.

- Understanding others' perspectives can help create stronger connections and reveal additional FUN in your interactions. Completing the exercises in this section provides you a more well-rounded perspective of what shapes others and will positively impact how you experience them.

- You determine your *next steps*. This is your journey to having more FUN in life. Self-reflection and honesty are key in maximizing the effectiveness of your strategy.

- The FUNdamentals of fundamism help bring additional joy and satisfaction to your life. To achieve this, you must find the FUNdamentals that connect with YOU.

- There area multiple ways to implement fundamism in your life. Whether you incorporate one new FUNdamental a day or one per week, or you try some other method, you must be patient with yourself. Creating behavioral change and shifting a mindset take time. Journal throughout the process, self-reflect regularly, and applaud yourself for hitting milestones in growth.

Next Up

In order to make FUN a staple in your life, to truly help you get through upcoming challenges and maximize life experiences, you have to continue your journey in what fundamism means to you.

In the next and final chapter, we'll tie a nice little bow on the concepts of fundamism while identifying what's next for you to drive sustainability and more FUN in your life!

Chapter 6
Game Time!!!

"Sometimes life knocks you on your ass... **Get up, get up, get up!!!** Happiness is not the absence of problems, it's the ability to deal with them."

—*Steve Maraboli*

WHAT TIME IS IT?!

GAME TIME!!!

It's been an extensive but exciting journey. We've explored the philosophy of fundamism, F.U.N., and the FUNdamentals to bring more joy and satisfaction to your life. You've spent time in self-reflection and even practiced many of the fundamism principles. Now it's game time.

In the days, weeks, months, and even years to follow, you'll experience challenge. How will you respond? Do you want to get over the challenge? Do you want to experience more fun in life, even with life's challenges?

Remember the story of Vinny Pazienza from chapter 1? "It's not that simple," people will tell you. You might even find yourself falling into the trap and saying it to yourself, "It's not that simple."

Don't believe it. You know better.

It *is* that simple. Do the thing they say can't be done, and it's done. Then you realize it is that simple, and it always was. You want a life characterized by joy? Create it. You want a life filled with FUN? Make it happen. You want a life of fulfillment where happiness is abundant and heartache finds you less and less? Stop doing the things that are creating the pain, and start doing more of the things that make you smile.

The answer is simple. Live the philosophy of fundamism and experience life through a lens that takes you beyond your wildest dreams. Find the FUNdamentals that lift you to a level you've always desired and gravitate towards all the things that give you strength.

Consistently make time to reflect and build upon your personal foundation. Leverage your understanding of others' perspectives to drive more meaningful relationships in your life, and create an evolving implementation strategy of next steps. This is the life of F.U.N.

Vince Lombardi, former head coach of the Green Bay Packers and one of the greatest leaders of our generation, once said, "I firmly believe that any man's finest hour, the greatest fulfillment of all that he holds dear, is that moment when he has worked his heart out in a good cause and lies exhausted on the field of battle—victorious."

Right now at this moment, choose to be the victor not the victim. Fight through the challenges that life throws at you and work your heart out to find the greatest fulfillment in all you hold dear. Let fundamism be your guide, the answer to all you seek in life.

Fun and real satisfaction are at your doorstep. Now go answer the freakin' bell and let the FUN begin!

Acknowledgments

Wow! We did it. Writing this book is one of my proudest moments in life, and it couldn't have been done without the help of many. This was truly a collaborative effort through stories, guidance, and support from my closest friends and family, and I'm eternally grateful for you all. I love you!

To my amazing wife, Melissa—you truly are the girl of my dreams. From the 5th grade on, I pictured myself with you, and your support has been paramount in the success of fundamism.

Brennan and Adalyn, the best children I could ask for—your humor, fun-loving attitudes, and kindness drive me more than you'll ever know. Every person, parent, and child should feel the genuine joy I see in your faces daily. Let that joy guide you in all you do, monkeys.

Mothers, Martha and Sandy—you two have been instrumental in my development. Your love, direction, and support (both monetarily, physically, and emotionally) have allowed me to take risks in life without fear of failure. Your value cannot be understated.

Chris, Jamie, and Cassie, my awesome siblings—you are all bosses! Never forget how truly special you are. We've had some amazing memories with many more to follow. Thank you for consistently voicing your admiration and appreciation for what I'm trying to accomplish. It drives me.

My guy, John Stoner! You've been my best friend from day one. From basketball to Prodigy, Desco, Slurpees, catsuits, and beyond—so many of my fondest experiences in life include you. I love you, bro. Thank you for always being there when I needed FUN the most.

I'm eternally grateful to have crossed paths and played a small role in the journey of Noah Wilson. Scott and Deb, from the bottom of my heart, I thank you. Your boy and our families' friendship made a huge impact on me. From now until I can no longer continue, I am committed to sharing the story of Noah and raising awareness for pediatric cancer research.

To my loving aunts, Carol and Elaine—you loved me as your own child for as long as I can remember. Your resilience through challenging times, light-heartedness, and willingness to share in all your fun played a direct role in creating my positive mindset. Props to you both.

Rod Johnson, you Lisa-Loeb-glasses-wearing stud! You were a mentor and guide at a pivotal moment in my life. You inspired confidence in me and were the business savvy, father figure I needed to reveal all the opportunities there are for someone to make an impact in this world. Thank you.

My Brotein Shake, Danny Duffy. Bruh. You've been on this journey with Noah's Bandage Project from the jump and you've made such an impact. You try your best to live by Gandhi's mantra, "Be the change you want to see in the world." I believe the world could benefit from more kindhearted, loving souls like you. Danny, you've made a difference to Scott, Deb, myself, and many others. Never underestimate all you've accomplished. I'm proud to call you my brother.

Chase McAnulty. I've always felt uncomfortable asking people for help. For one reason or another, you laid those fears to ease. I don't know why you decided to help me but you've played a major role in my success of late. I'm eternally grateful to have you in my life and appreciate your confidence in me. I look forward to pushing each other in the years to come while having all the FUN we can handle!

Travis Kelce—I'm so honored that you agreed to be a part of this project. Your spirit is the embodiment of fundamism, and I couldn't have asked for a better champion than you. You inspire so many in our community through your philanthropic efforts and authentic presence. From the bottom of my heart, thank you.

To the countless other friends and family that weren't mentioned above—you matter to me. The social media shares, thoughtful words, expressed confidence in my ability, and consistent pressure to push me forward have been instrumental in my success. I will never take your help for granted, and I look forward to our continued partnership in getting fundamism to the masses.

Finally, to my father, Sam. This is one of the hardest things I've ever said or written. I know you can't read this, but I can only hope you feel it wherever you are. While your life may not have ended up as you thought it would, you accomplished far more than you'll ever know. You created four beautiful children who aspire to make a difference in the lives of others—and we will because of you. Dad, our success is your success, so rest easy knowing that you were a catalyst in the inspiration of *fundamism*!

About the Author

Paul J. Long is a motivational speaker and consultant that has challenged the corporate landscape for over a decade and engaged audiences around the globe—all in the name of FUN! As the MLB Kansas City Royals' 2016 Fan of the Year, Paul's shenanigans have been featured in media outlets like ESPN, The Washington Post, and even The Wall Street Journal.

Through his concept of "fundamism" as well as his infectious spirit and unique take on F.U.N. in the workplace and life, Paul provides memorable experiences as a keynote speaker at hundreds of events a year. As president of the board of Noah's Bandage Project, Paul is an ardent champion of pediatric cancer research.

Paul challenges everyone to have FUN each and every day. So, what fun are you going to have today?

To learn more about Noah's Bandage Project, go to:

www.noahsbandageproject.com

To watch Paul speak, go to:

www.fundamism.com
www.pauljlong.com
Paul J Long on YouTube

*To learn more about fundamism and
join the fundamism community, go to:*

www.fundamism.com
@fundamism on Facebook
Paul J Long on YouTube

Want more Fundamism? Check out:

The Fundamism Podcast on
iTunes, Spotify, Google & Sticher Radio

To contact Paul, go to:

info@fundamism.com
Paul Long on LinkedIn
@fundamism on Facebook
@fundamismpaul on Twitter
@fundamismpaul on Instagram

Can you help?

Loved the book? Implemented *Fundamism* into your life?

If you did, I'd greatly appreciate you leaving an honest review of your experience on the Amazon page. Leaving a review will help more people find this book.

The more reviews a book has, the more relevant Amazon believes it is and the more likely they share it with the masses.

Thanks so much for your support, it means so much.

And don't forget to have F.U.N.!

Paul .J Long

Made in the USA
Middletown, DE
18 May 2019